MONEY
COME DANCE WITH ME

Gale West, MA, MFA

Table of Contents

Introduction

Healing our money relationship is one of the most powerful and essential things we can do for ourselves, both individually and collectively. This relationship with money permeates every aspect of our lives, including our connection to our self, our family, the marketplace and the planet. It is layered with the traumas and beliefs given to us by our families, our culture, our gender, class, and humanity as a whole.

These traumas and beliefs have held us hostage in constriction and lack. They have created structures that maintain the illusion of separation from one another and our divinity. As a result, those structures continue to perpetuate wars, create extremes of wealth and poverty, and destroy the land. Our planet, and life as we know it, is on the brink of extinction. Money, stuck in that system, has been hated, criticized, killed for, and sought after. Ultimately, it has been called the "root of all evil."

Is this money's fault, or rather, the result of an old paradigm of domination and greed that money got trapped in? Is it possible that money, as we know it, is actually a reflection of our collective souls, including both our shadow and our potential? Is it possible that healing both ourselves and money will open the door for a new paradigm to emerge? By facing, addressing, and changing our structures and systems around money, our true potential as divine creators can be revealed in our lives and in the world.

In my work with money as a consciousness, I have found its true essence to be an expansive, dynamic living force field of love connecting peoples, cultures, and marketplaces. When we bring our gifts and talents to the world, we share our time, magnificence and love. As a result, money becomes the expression of that love, allowing us the opportunity to care for ourselves and those we love, to share generously, and to participate in the banquet of life.

Mystics, ancients, indigenous peoples, and religious traditions have all predicted a golden era. They have spoken of a time of peace that is collaborative and generous, a time when the human family is just that—a *family* that honors the dignity of each member—and of a time when all of creation is honored and respected.

In my connections with indigenous shamans in Central and South America, I was told numerous stories of the prophecy of the eagle and the condor flying together in harmony. The eagle represents the people of the western world, bound by intellect and reason. The condor represents the indigenous peoples who live in connection to nature and the heart. In this prophecy, those bound by intellect (eagle) would bring the world to near extinction. But, a time would come when we would have the opportunity for the eagle and the condor to fly together, creating a new world where intellect and reason are guided by the wisdom of the heart. That time is now.

We stand poised at the precipice of choice. We can be agents for a new paradigm and a new dream, where decisions for ourselves and our planet are based on an economy that's sustainable and life affirming, collaborative and generous, or we can continue to support an economy that is based on domination and greed that no longer serves us or future generations.

We live in exciting times. Around the world people are making new choices, taking action and being agents for change. As more of us heal our relationship with money, the quicker it will ripple out into the quantum field, creating new possibilities for ourselves and our world.

Thank you for taking the journey!

The Dance

*"We should consider every day lost on which
we have not danced at least once."*

Fredrick Nietzsche

I am in Café Havana, the place for salsa dancing in Cartagena, Columbia. Even though the air conditioning is a relief from the steamy heat outside, inside there is a different heat. It is the heat of bodies and hips undulating together to a thumping rhythm. The music is loud. It invites everyone to move, to dance.

From my perch against the wall, I watch, mesmerized. Couples flow across the dance floor as if they are one instead of two, radiating grace and beauty.

My partner takes my hand. "Let's dance."

While I love to dance by myself, dancing with a partner has always brought anxiety. I think I won't know what to do. I'm afraid to trust my partner to lead in a way that is invitational and fun, instead of demanding. But tonight, the magic of the beat takes over and my feet move effortlessly. *We move as one.* The parts of me, worried that I didn't know how to dance, calm down. My body knows what to do. There is ease. The joy of the dance permeates into the core of my being. My heart is singing.

There is a gentle flow in trusting a dance partner that's similar to one's dance with money. Life can be delicious when inviting money, who is a willing partner, to the dance. But, by not trusting our partner we are, in essence, dancing alone. Trust, and we can surrender to the joy of the dance, knowing we will be fully supported and guided. Dancing, we become one with the flow of life.

The music ends. Holding hands, my partner and I walk out into the heat of the night. It is good.

CHAPTER 1

Money as Divine Source

"...most people, whether they realize it or not, are already in a deeply committed, unhappy relationship with their money."

Ken Honda, *Happy Money*

"Divine Source is a direct experience. So, no need to believe or disbelieve. Simply allow and... All is One"

Leland Lewis, *Random Molecular Mirroring*

What if you could have an amazing relationship with money? One that was free from anxiety, struggle and fear. What if that relationship could be a deep, intimate friendship that would guide and support you to dance together in a life filled with purpose, joy, and enough? Would you take it?

While it may seem strange to think you could actually have an intimate relationship with money, the truth is, you already do. Spouses, friends, bosses, jobs, or careers can come and go, but money will still be a prominent presence in your life, no matter how much you have or don't have.

Unfortunately, that relationship is often pretty dysfunctional. When I ask workshop participants to imagine honestly sharing with money their real feelings, many people are amazed at the intensity of sentiments coming from their mouth. Hatred, anger, hurt, contempt, despair, and powerlessness, just to name a few. One woman said to me, "No wonder I have a crappy relationship with money, I didn't realize how much hatred and anger I have towards it. If I were money, I wouldn't want to be around me, either."

It's bad enough to have all of our own adverse feelings around money, but adding ours to everyone else's only serves to create a radiating force field of negativity. Additionally, it's often difficult to differentiate what feelings are actually ours, versus what got passed down from our ancestors, plus what we've picked up in the general mush of society. Caught in the overwhelming tide of all of these feelings, it's easy to confuse the source of all our money frustrations as our own.

I often hear the adage, "Money is just energy." But, if money is just energy, how can it be the root of all evil, hateful, or worthy of contempt? These are feelings one has for a relationship, not energy.

Since we've established that you already have a relationship with money, having one that is joyful and expansive would be a whole lot more fun than one that is filled with fear, anger or angst. In all my years of guiding people to have a conscious relationship with money, what they've found is a loving and supportive presence, fostering healing, peace of mind, and an expanded trust in Divine Source.

Curiosity Opens the Door to New Realities

My own connection with money as a consciousness, was inspired by an insatiable curiosity and a lifelong passion to push beyond the limitations of my perception of reality by asking, "What is the greater truth?" As a child, I could see nature spirits and sensed a universe far beyond the one described to me in Catholic schools. As a result, I have an affinity for exploring concepts and points of view that are different from the western understandings of what is "real" that I grew up with. Interestingly, many of the concepts that our culture dismissed as "woo-

woo" a few years ago are now considered advanced science, particularly the in the realm of consciousness. [1]

My passion for truth led to many years of studying, teaching, and consulting in cutting-edge modalities in healing, human potential, psychotherapeutic techniques, and consciousness. This also included teaching business in Asia and the States. But one of the most powerful techniques I excelled at was accessing the quantum information field through something called the Akashic Records or Field, aka the A-Field.

Akasha is a Sanskrit word meaning "boundless space."[2] It is believed to be the building block of all creation. All information past, present, and future is considered to be imprinted in its field, including the history of all people, places, and things. Many religions and philosophies reference something similar using a different name, such as the *Book of Life* in Judaism. I like to tell my students that accessing it is sort of like drawing upon the 'Google' of the universe.

A number of years ago, the primary focus of my work was entrepreneurial coaching. I grew increasingly frustrated because there was often something we were missing, or not able to see, that was just beyond our conscious minds. One day I came across a quote in *The Immortal Mind* by Ervin Laszlo, who was twice nominated for a Nobel Prize in physics and is a strong advocate for the intersection between science, consciousness, and the Akashic Field:

"Consciousness is present in the mineral kingdom, in the living world, and in the social and ecological systems constituted by human beings."

---

1   For more information check out the Institute for Noetic Sciences, www.noetic.org, dedicated to the scientific study of consciousness.

2   For more information on the Akashic Records, read Ervin Laszlo's book, *Science and the Akashic Field*.

As I pondered this, it dawned on me that if this was true, then perhaps businesses had a consciousness that was separate from their owners. I wondered if it was possible to communicate with that consciousness through the Akashic Field. The answer was yes!

A bit tentatively, I approached my clients and fellow colleagues to "open" the Akashic Field of their businesses. What I found was that the business, indeed, a was separate entity with a consciousness that ached to grow, be of service, and had specific advice and wisdom for its owners. This was not only true for businesses, but also non-profits. Unfortunately, the businesses were often frustrated with the ways their owners were unconsciously stifling their growth.

Over time, I began to realize that one of the primary issues affecting a business's growth was often the entrepreneur's relationship with money, typically fraught with limitation and fear. That relationship was unconsciously being projected on to the business, limiting its growth and income potential. Since money seemed to be the root of many problems, I started to wonder if money also had a consciousness and if it was possible to communicate with it, too, through the Akashic Field.

Discovering a Loving Presence

One cold March morning, sitting on my comfy black couch, pen and paper in hand, my conversation with money started like this: "Dear money, how do you grow?"

Amazingly, I heard a voice in my head saying, *"By investing in stocks, bonds, companies, and yourself. In many ways, I grow exponentially. I expand to meet the needs of the people, society and culture.*

"If I am considered bad, I will be used in ways that are not in alignment with the society's highest and best. But consider Costa Rica. This is an example of a country that is not living in fear or lack. It has no need to

expend me [money] to maintain an army. It is a country that utilizes its beauty, climate, natural resources and sunshine for good. As a result, it is an expansive place to be and a force field for growth."

I was stunned! These were not only words I would never say, but even more so, I hadn't ever considered Costa Rica from this perspective. More than seventy years ago, Costa Rica disbanded its military. The money previously allocated for weapons and maintaining an army was now used to help its citizens enjoy a better life. Today it is one of the most flourishing countries in Central America. Money was right, it doesn't live in fear.

Money went on to say: *"Unfortunately, America is expanding into a country of haves and have-nots. It has become a nation that is divisive, secretive and fear-based. Even though its principles are based on freedom, people do not feel freedom from fear, anger and inequality.*

"It is wrong to think that I do not have a consciousness. I do. I am more than just energy transferred. I want to grow. I want to flow. I want to be an agent for good."

OMG, this was amazing! What I had just experienced was a presence, distinct and profound. As a result of that initial conversation, I began to communicate with money daily. I was curious. This dialogue was different than anything I had ever experienced. What I found was a loving presence that wanted me to be happy, to open my ability to receive, to choose joy, to flourish, to know that I was enough and that there was a place for my gifts in the marketplace.

If anyone had told me I would be talking to money and traveling around the world teaching others to talk to money, I would have said, "I don't think so." My Catholic background did not include having conversations with money. I was taught the old maxim that it's easier for a camel to go through the eye of a needle than a rich man to go to heaven. While this proverb supposedly has nothing to do with literal needles, the message was pretty clear: *God and wealth do not go together!*

Yet, as my connection to the consciousness of money deepened, I realized that I was developing a powerful relationship with something greater than myself. This Presence, which identified as Money, had an almost angelic quality that was definitely spiritual and so different from what I'd been taught to believe. Money was helping me heal deep wounds that were beyond mere money, and at the same time, affecting my ability to receive it.

A Playful and Expansive Being

In his landmark book, *Think and Grow Rich,* Napoleon Hill invites the audience to call upon an Infinite Intelligence for guidance and support. Connecting with money as a consciousness could be tapping into this greater Intelligence that Hill speaks of. As someone with a mystical orientation deeply rooted in practicality, I've come to believe that my communications have actually been with Divine Source manifesting through money. Divine Source can manifest as many things, but since money is our primary method of exchange, it would make sense that It would want us to experience money with greater ease and grace during our human experience.

Over the years, what I've found is that this divine essence, expressed as the soul of money, will appear in distinct ways unique to what each person needs. In the beginning I never saw an image; I only felt a presence that was distinctly male.

One day, while working on last-minute tweaks for a weekend money retreat, a large being whose essence was filaments of light appeared. It sported a shimmering cloak made of gold, and glided through space, showering sparkling gold dust everywhere. Intuitively, I knew this luminous being represented the divine essence of money, radiating lightness, delight, joy, and unconditional love. Awed at the beauty of this image, I felt a deep sense of gratitude at having been gifted with this vision.

Later in this book, you will have the opportunity to create your own connection with money as a loving guide and friend.

An Invitation to Dance

While the concepts in this book may be novel, as you begin to dance with money you will find it guiding you to create a joyously wealthy life that is rich with connection, options, fulfillment, joy and delight. It will reconnect you to your heritage as a co-creator of your life with the Divine. You will begin to dream a new dream of your interconnectivity with all of creation.

It doesn't matter how much money you have, if your relationship with money is fraught with anxiety, lack, devoid of meaning, or just plain sucks, this book is for you. My commitment in writing it is to bring healing to the deep wounds so many of us carry, including our current paradigm around money.

Together we will explore and heal our stories and perceptions around money. You will have your own connection with the divine essence of Money as a guide and invite it to come dance with you. You will reconnect to your own divine essence as the predominant creative force in your life; expand your ability to listen to your heart's true desire and open yourself to joyously receive life's bounty. As you move from unconscious to conscious spending and honoring your gifts, Money will aid you in the journey to peace, trust and ease.

There are many stories of the transformation from the personal prison of struggle to freedom of self; from deep feelings of lack and worthlessness to an abundance of love, tranquility, and worth; from insecurity, to trusting in a Divine Source that is generous and life affirming.

Note on capitalization: As we journey together, the word money will bring many meanings that I may or may not articulate. I think you will be able to distinguish between *money* in its physical form and *Money* as a consciousness in the context of the text.

Let's dance!

Dance Steps:

Write a letter to Money. Honestly share with Money how you truly feel about it, the wounds you've experienced around it, and anything else you want to share regarding your current relationship.

When you feel complete, share with Money the relationship you would like to have.

Dancing with
the Stories

CHAPTER 2

Money's Story

"Money is like love; it kills slowly and painfully the one who withholds it and enlivens the other who turns it on his fellow man."

Kahlil Gibran

One morning, in my daily communication with Money, I heard these words:

The predominant matrix of humanity has been domination and greed. I have been aligned to that. The new matrix of humanity is collaboration and generosity. I want to be aligned to that. Can you please help me?

I was stunned by what this message implied: that Money had been wounded as much as we had been wounded by money. We were not the only victims in this old system—money was too. But, what was even more profound was that even though it was stuck in an old paradigm, a new one was emerging. And money had the inside scoop on what it was. Money wanted its freedom!

Years ago, I went camping with friends. The only toilet available was a wooden outhouse on the edge of campground. As I entered the tiny structure, I walked into the stench of many who had visited before me. Unfortunately, when finished and reaching for my flashlight, it slipped out of my hand and fell into the hole. I stared down into the now illuminated, fetid slime of human excrement. My flashlight was beyond liberation! As I walked away, I looked back at the little wooden building emanating an eerie glow. I saw people hesitate before they walked in, surprised by the light flowing out into the darkness. In the morning, I went to check on my flashlight. I held my nose and gingerly peered down the hole. Even though my flashlight was now covered, the light was still shining.

Money is like that flashlight—desperately attempting to emanate its light, but stuck at the bottom of the outhouse of our collective "stuff."

How Money Is Wounded

If money has been linked to a paradigm of domination and greed, then it follows that it has become an agent for the perpetuation of that paradigm. Locked in a prison that has become increasingly controlled by a select few, it has been employed to promote what former economist and shaman, John Perkins,[3] describes as a "death economy" instead of a "life economy." As a result, Earth has been raped to grow it and many have prostituted themselves in order to obtain it. Money's been blamed for the pain and suffering that has been perpetrated in its name. There is enough, there is more than enough, yet one person dies every four seconds of hunger. Money no longer wants to participate. It wants its liberation and redemption. But money needs our healing before it can be freed.

In my money workshops, I draw a vertical line down a big sheet of paper. I invite participants to brainstorm all the ways money has been wounded and it has wounded us. Words such as war, bloodshed, greed, hunger, trauma, the destruction of the planet, pain, poverty, and unrelenting consumption fill the left side of the paper.

The next question we explore is, what could money facilitate if it was allowed to be an agent for good? On the right side of the paper are words like art,

---

3   Author of *New York Times* Bestseller, *Confessions of an Economic Hit Man*

expansion, creativity, ideas, enough, safety, generosity, collaboration, reverence for all life, healthcare, education and a healthy planet.

The list of wounds feels heavy and despairing. In contrast, the list of money's potential radiates excitement, aliveness and hope.

Money's Origins

Even though the message of many religious institutions is that money is evil, the earliest forms of money, such as cowry shells, were considered to be sacred objects. Cowry shells, in some traditional African religions, are still used in sacred ceremony.

While visiting the money museum in Istanbul, I was stunned to see beautiful religious symbols on one side of a coin and a secular symbol on the other, the inference being that money was an intersection between the human and the Divine. It was an agent for the Divine to support us while existing in the "marketplace" of our human state.

While bartering is still a valuable form of exchange, the move from barter to money enabled communities to grow and expand through the exchange of cultures, goods and ideas. Herbs and spices from one place brought new flavors for food to another. Dyes brought new patterns and beauty to clothes. Silks from China brought soft textures and delight to its wearers.

A relationship of trust and integrity with money was, and still is, integral in the barter economy. In many Asian cultures, it is considered rude to talk about money before a relationship has been established. Lots of tea or beer must be consumed, food shared, and trust established before any business or money is discussed. It is understood that, while the exchange is a tangible thing, it is people who are still at the center of that exchange. Relationships and people matter.

Money has had many incarnations, from cowry shells and beads, to precious metal coins, to today's most common manifestation in paper. As we humans shift and grow, money's forms shift and grow with us. Increasingly, around the world, banks, as holding tanks for money, do not exist. In Africa, for example, you might find kiosks that will allow you to send money to someone's cell phone. I can open an app on my phone and money is transferred. According to my friends in China, even street vendors take Alipay.

It doesn't matter how what we call money is exchanged. In many ways, it's a reflection of what we value that determines what something will cost. If we collectively decide that something has a lot of value, its price will reflect that. If together we decide that something has no value, it may be hard to even give it away. The stock market fluctuates based on perceptions of possible expansion or contraction. Much of it is based on fear or optimism. All of this is to say, our collective thoughts and expectations are the drivers of money's bus. If we collectively decide that guns have no value to us as a society, they either won't be made or will be hard to sell.

A Vast Web of Connection

For most of us, the relationship between what we buy, and those who made it possible for us to purchase it, has been lost. I typically don't consider that the bouquet of roses I purchased at the grocery store might have come from a rose farm in Ecuador, thousands of miles away. Unconsciously I pick it up, toss it in my metal cart, and head to the check out with the rest of my groceries that may have traveled almost as far.

Consider a loaf of bread: The money you paid for that bread has been distributed to many, many people. Included in this interaction are the seeds, the farmer, the equipment needed to plant and harvest the grain, all of the people who made that equipment, including those who made the parts and those who assembled it, the raw materials to make the parts, which may have come from all over the world, the mill that ground the grain, the paper bags the flour is packaged in, the trees that were used to make the paper, the factory that created the bags, the bakery that put all of the ingredients together, including the bakers and the ovens, the yeast that was used for the bread to rise, the people and vehicles used to transport the bread, the plastic bags used to package the bread, which came from oil pumped in another country and shipped to the factory to make the bags, the person in the grocery store who put the bread on the shelf, the person who checked you out, and the bagger who put it a bag. All of this for a loaf of bread!

One day, I was sitting in my home pondering the numerous money exchanges that had probably taken place that day. It dawned on me that *everything* around me was there as a result of an exchange of money, down to the nails in the wall. I wondered if the all the money exchanged had been happy or not. Had all the interactions been good? Were the people involved treated well and paid fairly? Was the energy of all the interactions still radiating in the space? I had a new appreciation for the continuous flow of money and its impact in every interchange that involves it.

It's easy to forget that when we buy something that our money has touched many people. If money is the expression of divine love in the marketplace, then all of these people brought a piece of themselves to their work. In any exchange, be it money or barter, there are numerous interactions involved. Taking time to consider all the hours and the lives of those who have given their time, ingenuity, creativity, and skill, and the resources used to bring you the things you are buying can be humbling.

Envisioning a New Paradigm for Money

Money enables us to inhabit a world that has increasingly become a global village. It allows us to connect people and cultures. In China, previously impoverished farmers are now flourishing as their beautiful flowers are brought to a New York sidewalk market. Local farmers in Guatemala are creating cooperatives to bring their coffee to international markets.

Continuing to chain Money to the shackles of the old paradigm of domination and greed assures that we will forever remain imprisoned in that world. If Money is our creation, then we are no better than how we use it, create it, or distribute it. Helping Money heal, holding a vision for its pure potential as the expression of divine love in the marketplace, and reconnecting to our own divinity is the key to creating a new relationship with Money, not only for ourselves individually, but also collectively.

Invocation for Money's Healing

The following invocation recognizes how Money has been wounded and calls forth a new reality for Money to step into. It invites Money to be its true divine essence. As Money heals, we heal.

Money, you've been our servant, now be our friend.
Money, we have wounded you, as you have wounded us.
I come now to give you the healing we both need.

Money, you have been forced to cause tears of sorrow, now inspire tears of joy.

Money, you have been forced to cause the fires of rage, now bring forth the fires of inspiration,

Money, you have been forced to cause the parched ground of poverty, now become the fertile ground of prosperous wholeness,

Money, you have been forced to be a facilitator of abuse, now facilitate generosity and delight,

Money, you have been forced to cause spiritual chains, now become a creator of spirit.

Money, reveal yourself as an expression of divine love.
Money, reveal yourself as bringer of justice and balance.
Money, reveal yourself as a being that facilitates happiness and joy.
Money, you are now healed, cleansed and whole. We are both free.

Dance Steps

Over this next week consider including the invocation in your daily prayers. Imagine money, the collective, and yourself being cleansed and healed.

Bring more awareness to your shopping experience by imagining all of the people who brought their time, energy and talents to the purchases you are making. Gift them with your gratitude and blessings.

CHAPTER 3

The Stories of the Collective

"Every gun that is made, every warship launched,
every rocket fired signifies, in the final sense, a theft from those
who hunger and are not fed, those who are cold and are not
clothed. This world in arms is not spending money alone."

President and General Dwight D. Eisenhower

Our Collective Imprints

A few years ago, I was traveling with friends through Vietnam and Cambodia. We'd decided to go by boat down the Mekong River from Ho Chi Min City to Phnom Pen. Ho Chi Min City had been teeming with vibrancy, intense heat, noise and new opportunities. Floating on the swift current, all that intensity was replaced by bucolic scenes. We passed water buffalo languidly eating the tall grasses that lined the river banks and waved to an occasional gaggle of children who seemed delighted to be acknowledged.

Our boat docked at a small wooden plank that led to an outdoor restaurant at the border. We waited while our Vietnamese guide set out to get the requisite visas needed for Cambodia.

Returning, she led us down a little dirt path along the river's edge. I stepped over a small rope that served as the border crossing.

Immediately, an overwhelming sense of heaviness descended upon me. I felt deep grief and sadness. My friend, Nick, a tall brash Texan, looked at me inquiringly, "Did you feel that?"

"You felt that?" I asked incredulously.

All we did was step over a rope! It was such a contrast from my experience of Vietnam, which felt vibrantly expansive and hopeful. The pain and grief of genocide the people of Cambodia had experienced so many years ago was still palpable in the land of that country, miles from where it happened. While Vietnam has definitely had its own past traumas, it is possible that my experience was evidence of the degree of energetic healing of both countries.

This incident in Cambodia imprinted in me a profound understanding of how collective pain is so deep that can be etched, not only in our psyches, but even into the land.

Similarly, our collective money wounds are long and deep. These wounds are reflected in the very fabric of our societies. The traumas perpetrated, in the name of money, create the paradigms and lens of our perceptions of truth.

The High Price of Inequality

In their groundbreaking book, *The Spirit Level*, Richard Wilkinson and Kate Pickett explore the effects of economic inequality on societies. While it is true that those on the bottom of the economic ladder are more profoundly affected, statistically, everyone is impacted and the cost is high. As Wilkinson and Pickett write: "Across whole populations, rates of mental illness are five times higher in the most unequal compared to the least unequal societies… people are five times more likely to be imprisoned, six times more likely to be clinically obese, and murder rates are higher."[4]

In many countries, inequity is often based on deep racial and class bias. As a result, the opportunities available to one group of people are not readily or easily available to others. Being in a society that values one group of people more than another only serves to rob us of our collective potential.

---

4   Wilkinson and Pickett, p176

Returning to the States after living and traveling abroad for almost five years, I observed my own country with fresh eyes, like those of an outsider. Instead of a democracy, I saw a country controlled by special interest groups and large companies who used money and influence for their own benefit without considering the cost to the common good. I saw social injustice and inequity in a way I hadn't seen before. I saw how our misplaced assumption that this is the land of opportunity has kept us blind to the inequity that is infused into the very fabric of our society. Pretending that something does not exist does not make us immune to its effects.

We are not immune to the impact of the struggles of those less fortunate than us, even though we may not be conscious of it. I am always amazed at how many people I've worked with who live in fear of being a "bag lady," or a homeless man living in a van under a bridge down by the river. Often this private fear is a dominant cause of anxiety for highly educated, well-paid people.

We are like fish, unaware that we are swimming in the unconscious water of our cultural norms around money and success. They are ever-present in our psyche as "that's the way it is." As a result, they become unexamined and taken for truth.

The Collective Prison of "Not Enough"

In many of our collective money stories, the subtle message is that our value and worth are defined by financial success. Thus, those with more money have more value and wield more power; and those at the bottom of the society's financial rung have less value and often, no voice. As a result, our intrinsic sense of value and worth is often influenced by where we are on the status and financial acquisition rung. But, at what expense to our self and our souls?

Collectively, too many of us are locked in the prison of constantly needing to prove or posture our worth. This results in more inequity, which breeds less caring, which breeds less mutuality, which breeds more competition, which breeds less trust, which breeds insecurity, which breeds more fear, which breeds more powerlessness, which breeds more anger, which breeds more anxiety, which breeds a more alienated society, which breeds more alienation from ourselves. Wow, that's intense!

No matter how much we have, there will always be someone with more. Comparison and status anxiety are often the price of higher and higher incomes, producing a sort of poverty of the soul, keeping people in the prison of lifestyles, jobs, marriages, and situations that hold them hostage to an image they have to maintain in order to prove that they have value and worth by standards set from the outside.

The free-floating anxiety I struggled with for years could never ease because no matter how productive I was, it was never enough. I once proclaimed to a friend that I was a closet type A personality. He replied, "You're not in the closet!" I was chagrined to realize that what I thought was my personal little secret wasn't a secret after all.

> *The stress that comes with society's obsession with accomplishment and acquisition as a measure of status levies a huge toll on all of us!*

My friend Jeanne shared the story about the beautiful spring day she made a conscious decision to push money away:

I was sitting in my back yard, looking out at the swimming pool, manicured lawn and garden. I had everything. I had the large, lavishly furnished house, the handsome man and a lifestyle that anyone would envy. In that moment, I realized I was not happy. I looked around at the people I knew,

24

people in my neighborhood. I knew a lot of them were not happy, either. But they were stuck because of the money. Stuck in marriages, in jobs, and in trying to maintain a lifestyle that cost them dearly. I made a vow that I would never again let money figure prominently in my life.

For the next twenty years, I pushed money away. I wanted nothing to do with it. I realize now that it was not money's fault. I blamed money for my unhappiness and for those around me. Money didn't do anything wrong. Being able to think of money as having a consciousness who gets blamed for so much has helped me to invite it back into my life again. It feels good.

So many of the people in my life, including me, were stuck trying to prove we were enough but were actually victims of our own making.

While it can seem difficult not to be influenced by our collective cultural values, it's not impossible. We can begin to choose to dance with money on our own terms. Creating a relationship with money that reconnects us to our divinity and intrinsic worth helps to heal the deep wounds we all hold. When there is nothing to prove, we are finally free to a create life that aligns with our divine path and purpose.

When a tipping-point of the population has shifted their personal paradigms to ones that are soul enhancing, our collective paradigms will change. Knowing that our intrinsic value and worth has nothing to do with our place in society opens the door to a world where the intrinsic value of *all* is acknowledged and celebrated. As a result, *everyone* benefits. Money is free to be an agent for the good of all, not just a chosen few.

Dance Steps

Over the next week, bring mindfulness to the subtle messages of ads, pictures, images, and comments around money and success. What are they telling you about who is important and who is not, who has value and who doesn't? How might they be affecting you and your attitude toward yourself and others? Notice without judgment, but with compassion.

Money loves generosity*! Donate to a cause you care about. Consider giving to an organization that is dedicated to promoting social or economic justice.*

CHAPTER 4

The Stories of the Ancestors

*"If you look deeply into the palm of your hand, you will see
your parents and all generations of your ancestors. All of them
are alive in this moment. Each is present in your body. You are
the continuation of each of these people."*

Thich Nhat Hanh, *Present Moment Wonderful Moment*

The Legacy Burdens of Our Ancestors

I got a call from a client one day who was crying, "Why does money
hate me? It seems no matter what I do, I'm always struggling."

"Money doesn't hate you," I replied. "It really isn't capable of hating
you. I think the bigger issue is that you have an alignment with struggle.
Do you have any idea where you might have gotten that from?"

She gasped, "Oh my God, financial struggle is so core to my family's
experience. It goes back generations. I don't remember a time my family
didn't struggle with money."

Guiding her into her ancestral timeline, my client intuitively connected
with an ancient ancestor who was exceptionally poor and had to steal
food to keep from starving. The trauma of that life became imprinted
into her family's collective memory. As a result, there were four other
generations where struggle predominated, including her mother's and
ultimately hers. We unburdened and cleared the energetic pattern of
financial struggle from her ancestors.

The next day she sent a note saying, "Today, I woke up with a peace I have never felt before. I can't explain it. So unexpected, so calm, so smooth and lovely. Thank you."

What my client thought was her fate in life was merely a manifestation of what those who'd lived before her had experienced. The stories of our ancestors' traumas become imprinted in the genetic code of our families, passed down from generation to generation. These ancestral legacy burdens are energetic imprints that hold the information, beliefs and feelings from the traumatic experiences of our ancestors. Even though these imprints are not our own traumas, they inhabit our energy field and unconsciously influence our thoughts and behaviors. Unfortunately, they become part of our identity because we don't realize that the narrative isn't our own, but instead, the family story.

While exploring my own ancestral money trauma, I'd assumed that the majority of it was passed down from my mother. She was left with five young children and minimal governmental support after my father died. But once when I asked her if she ever worried about money, she looked at me quizzically. "No, I never worried about money. I always trusted there would be enough." Since that was not my own experience around money, I wondered where else it might have come from.

I had no idea that even though my father had died when I was four, it was his family's trauma that I was unconsciously carrying, not my mother's. His parents had taken advantage of a government program designed to populate remote areas of the country by cheaply selling previously owned Native American land. Instead of the promised land they thought they were getting, the terrain offered nothing but drought, hardship and extreme poverty. As the oldest of the family, it was my father's job to convince the local grocer to exchange eggs for pencils for him and his school-age siblings. This was their level of poverty.

I was surprised to discover that deeply imbedded in my genetic code was the money trauma of my father's ancestral lineage, despite the fact that I have very few actual memories of him. Interestingly, those memories have nothing to do with money. Still, his DNA is part of my own.

Christel Nani's book, *Sacred Choices: Thinking Outside the Tribe to Heal Your Spirit*, makes a strong case for the importance of identifying family beliefs and stories as a path to healing. She gives numerous examples of transformational shifts as a result of disengaging from disempowering family beliefs. We don't have to continue to carry our family traumas and legacies.

In my money retreats, we often trace the outline of each participant's body on a large piece of paper. I lead them into a trance state, inviting them to connect to the energetic ancestral burdens held in or on their body. On the paper map of their body, they draw the legacy burdens they're sensing energetically. For many, it's an incredibly powerful experience to both feel and see the burdens in a life-sized visual representation, evoking compassion and understanding for themselves and their ancestors.

The idea that family traumas are inherited is a relatively new concept, but one seriously studied in the science of epigenetics.[5] Additionally, the cutting-edge psychotherapeutic model of Internal Family Systems (IFS) recognizes that ancestral burdens have a significant impact. IFS offers methods for clearing them that I'll share later in this chapter.

Collective Traumas Become Our Family's Trauma

Traumas that groups of people experience will create a collective response, but are also uniquely imprinted into each individual family's

---

5   https://www.bbc.com/future/article/20190326-what-is-epigenetics

story. An example of a collective trauma is the depression of the 1930's, which was experienced both in the States and in Europe. It was relentless and affected people across all classes, lasting 10 long years in the States. Many people lost their entire savings when the banks closed and the stock market crashed. Destitute and often homeless, people roamed the country in search of work.

A workshop participant shared that her mother's family lost their farm during the depression and almost starved to death. She then came to understand that the terror and fear of lack that colored her life was not hers. Even so, it resulted in her clinging tightly to money except when buying food, as she had a compulsion to make sure her refrigerator was full. When she realized the reason behind her obsession with a full refrigerator, she laughed. "I could never make sense of my fixation with food. Funny, my mother was the same way. I hadn't made the connection with her family almost starving. I have so much compassion for myself and my family and feel a sense of freedom now that I understand. "

I used to think my mother's fixation on potatoes was strange until I realized she, too, went through the depression. She grew up on a farm, and while they didn't lose it, there were still lean years of drought. She used to say, "At least we had potatoes." Potatoes became the staple that fed their family through the long years that the depression had its grip on the country. Potatoes meant staying alive.

Similarly, the extreme disturbances of war, genocide, or the mass forced exodus of groups of people result in both collective and family traumas. These experiences and how family members interpret them as far as life, money, and what is possible, will be energetic imprints in our own fields.

For example, Jerry's grandparents were Irish immigrants who came to America because of the potato famine. In his own words: "My whole family is very serious. We have a difficult time enjoying life and feel more comfortable with struggle. I had no idea how much my grandparents' experience has affected me in so many ways."

As in Jerry's case, often the traumas of our grandparents become the deep imprints in the family legacy. It helps to know that most of the disempowering beliefs you carry around money and life aren't yours!

Legacy Burdens of Religious Traditions

A woman raised her hand in a workshop and said, "How am I supposed to have a positive relationship with money when my whole life I've been told that it's evil?

"You're right," I replied. "Thankfully you're an adult now. You get to choose what you want to believe and what you don't. Is it possible to consider that it's not true that money is evil, but that this is just an old belief given to you, which isn't serving you anymore? Let's deconstruct where the old one came from and give you the freedom to decide what you want instead."

I'm sure there are a number of you reading this book who received a similar message from parents and/or religious institutions. Since we live in world where money is the means of exchange, defining money as evil produces a lot of dysfunctional behavior. We need money to function in the world, but aren't supposed to want it. That is way too crazy making!

The natural extension of this thinking is that spiritual people shouldn't care about money. This becomes extrapolated into a belief that those doing "spiritual work" shouldn't charge. But, if this is the gift you bring to the marketplace, how are you to live? The result is: charging brings guilt, undercharging brings resentment. This is not a recipe for spirituality.

My friend Amy's first job out of ministerial school paid her $28,000 a year. In her own words, "I had two master's degrees, and yet I didn't feel as if it was okay to ask for more. I was raised by hippie parents and a traditional Christian message that money was evil and bad. I felt guilty for wanting more.

I now realize that God's work is Divine work, and as such, deserves to be paid. Money is not evil, but an avenue for God to bring us all that we need to be generous with ourselves and others."

Honestly, the world needs more spiritual people with money. Here is a fascinating quote from the Baha'i faith with a very different message than is common in many religious traditions: "Wealth is praiseworthy in the highest degree, if it is acquired by an individual's own efforts and the grace of God, in commerce, agriculture, art and industry and if it be expended for philanthropic purposes."[6]

Legacy Burden of Struggling Creatives

Beyond ancestral and religious challenges, different industries will have their own money burdens. Similar to the spiritual person who is supposed to not ask for or want money, people in creative industries can also hold burdens of struggle and poverty. In certain countries, creatives are relished and appropriately compensated. In others, particularly in America, that is often not the case. The other day I overheard an artist say, "No one wants their child to study art." While this might not be totally true, it's true enough. There are way too many stories of financially struggling artists whose paintings sell for millions after their deaths.

Artists, musicians, performers, writers and other creatives are the divine sparks that advance our civilizations and, as such, deserve to be paid for the gifts they bring to the world. They imbue beauty, inspiration, awe and healing into the collective field. They connect us to joy, delight, play

---

6   *The Secret of Divine Civilization*, Abdu'l-Baha

and the divinely human urge for expression. Without the creatives of the world, it would be a dark, bleak place to live in.

Clearing the legacy burden of creative financial struggle opens the door for options, opportunities, and inventive and creative ways to invite money to dance.

Allowing for Release

It's important to realize that most of the dysfunction in your money relationship is not your fault. It came from somewhere else. More than likely your grandparents. You are not bad, stupid, or any other unkind thing you might say to yourself. There are tools for healing that were not available for your ancestors.

These ancestral and collective burdens are often trapped in our root chakra, which is located at the base of the spine. Our root chakra is our connection to being in a body and the world of form. When the root chakra is stuck, it is difficult to create our lives with ease instead of struggle. This is why I'm passionate about clearing ancestral burdens as one of the first tasks I undertake with people. Life will give us enough to work with on its own. It's an act of loving kindness for all concerned to heal and release what is not yours to carry anymore, healing and clearing the pain, hurt and disappointment of the generations that went before us. As we heal, they heal. Additionally, it is not only essential to unburden our ancestors, but also the energetic patterns and beliefs no longer serving us from alliances, communities, and institutions with which we've been connected.

Being able to clear your ancestral burdens requires enough mindfulness to notice the patterns in your family and be willing to disconnect from them. It is a gift to yourself, your family, and the collective field.

Dance Steps

Meditation for Healing and Clearing Ancestral Burdens

This exercise may not clear all of your ancestral burdens, but it is a place to start. I recommend reading it through, or recording it, before you actually do the clearing. For a free recording of this meditation, go to moneycomedancewithme.com

Imagine one of your parents, or a primary childhood caretaker, in front of you. (If you feel uncomfortable with him/her, you can imagine a protective shield around you.) Tune into your body and notice what negative feelings you're feeling regarding money or life that you received from your parent or caregiver.

Your ancestors might have given you different imprints, depending on their trauma. Just feel into the feelings. Fear, guilt, shame, burden, sacrifice, "life is hard," etc.

Imagine putting these feelings or beliefs in a ball of energy or container in front of you. Once you've put all of the negative feelings you've received from your parent or caretaker into the energy ball or container, hand it back to them. Invite them to hand it back to whomever they received it from. Continue to see it handed back along the generational lines. Invite the last person to give all of these burdens to the light to be transmuted and transformed. Bathe your whole ancestral lineage with light and healing. Know that whether they are dead or alive, you've invited healing for all your ancestors. Bless them and send them on their way.

Repeat with your other parent, and then, from whomever else you are holding burdens until the process feels complete. Consider spouses or partners whose burdens you may have unconsciously taken on.

Additionally, are there any other burdens from religious alliances, organizations or groups that you are ready to release? Take time to do that now, giving them to the light to be transmuted and transformed.

Once completed, imagine standing under a waterfall of beautiful healing light. Filling the spaces those burdens took up. Bring blessings and healing to all concerned.

Is there a new empowering paradigm of belief you want to incorporate into your life? If so, write it down and use it as an affirmation for the next 30 days.

Note: *From your father, or the primary breadwinner, you may find a heavy burden of financial responsibility on your shoulders. It may appear as a cloak to be removed.*

From mothers, you may find a legacy burden of other people's needs being more important and/or the feeling that it's not okay to ask for what you need. Another common theme from mothers is unfulfilled dreams, particularly if the mother gave up her dreams to raise children.

CHAPTER 5

Our Inner Children's Stories

"The past is a script we are constantly rewriting. "

Michael Moorcock

"The only decision we get to make is what role we'll play in our own lives. Do we want to write this story or do we want to hand the power over to someone else?"

Brene' Brown, *Rising Strong*

In the last chapter we explored our legacy burdens from ancestors and institutions. Now it's time to look at our own stories and the childhood memories that are still lingering in our psyches.

As children, we absorb the feelings that radiate in our home, both the negative and positive. These include our primary caregiver's constructs, from their personal experiences and those of their own parents. We see how they struggle, what they do, how they spend and how they relate to money and life. Our parents' stories of losses endured, who is revered and why, are all part of our personal legacy. They make up the world we know to be true and our expectations of what is possible for us to have and to be.

Our childhood memories become the narratives that create the reality and lens of our lives. Our identity consists of the conclusions we make about ourselves and our world. We create parts designed to protect our inner children from harm by attempting to manage our outer world. All too often, their strategies are limited to what worked best in childhood.

I grew up in a home where hard work was extolled and leisure was frowned upon. Being sick was considered just an excuse to not work. As the second oldest of eleven, I spent my childhood taking care of children. Witnessing abuse or being abused by my stepfather was always a possibility, because anything could trigger him. As a child, I unconsciously concluded that if I did something for no other reason than it brought me joy, I could be punished. Since work was extolled and joy was not, the message became: The only way to make money is to do things I don't want to do.

I had no idea these beliefs were operating in my life until I began to explore the patterns that consistently showed up by asking, "What must I believe for this to be my reality?"

For many years I was constantly focusing on work, which didn't include taking time for what brought me joy. Even though my work as a psychotherapist was profound for many people, at the end of the day, I often heard a voice saying, "Other people get to have a life, but I don't." I was still taking care of children. But this time, it was the inner children of my clients. I was good at making money, but stuck in my small box of how to make it.

The two beliefs were so intertwined, they created a reality that had few options. Uncovering them helped me to understand the despair and hopelessness I'd felt for many years.

Asking the parts of me who still held the traumatic memories how they wanted to rewrite their story brought a surprising answer. In my hometown, there was a children's home with a large green lawn, big climbing trees and beautiful horses to ride. As a child it was my dream to live there instead of the bleak white house of my childhood.

In my new story, this is where all my inner children wanted to live. I changed the name to a "Home for Children." In this place, the adults were safe and kind. I didn't have to take care of anyone. I had my own room, and there was a Waldorf school that was rich with intellectual and creative stimulation.

When I shared with my partner that my inner children were now happily living in the home for children, he was shocked. "You put your inner children in an orphanage?"

"Oh no, it's a wonderful place. It's a home. It has all of the things I ached to have as a child. It's a safe place to happily be me!"

Creating a new story opened my unconscious mind to new possibilities and a new empowering paradigm: "It is safe to be happy and do things just because they bring me joy. It is my right and the joy of the Creator."

Once this new paradigm was fully anchored into my reality, I created another one for money: "Money is my friend and wants to come to me in ways that are fulfilling, delightful, make my heart sing, and are perfectly aligned with my gifts, purpose, how and who I am called to serve. Money and I dance together."

Changing my story changed my reality. Since in the unconscious mind there is no time, it also changed my history. There was a new imprint in the timeline of my life that included a different possibility. No longer locked in the past, I created a parallel life that informs this one and will continue to inform it as I fill the new life with luscious, vivid images that are happy, safe, and joyful.

Childhood Conclusions of Truth

Little children will often assume responsibility for the actions of the adults in their world, concluding that everything that happens must be their fault. The resulting conclusions are often, "I'm too much." "I'm not enough." "I'm flawed." "I'm not loveable." "It's not safe to be fully alive."

Or in my case, "It's not safe to be happy." These are just some of the many overlays that become our identity.

These conclusions about ourselves will determine the neighborhoods we feel comfortable in, the people we fit with, the sense of possibility we allow for ourselves, how we treat others, the sacrifices we are willing to make for our dreams, and what we feel that we deserve or don't deserve. These choices affect numerous areas of our lives.

Jared, a *Course in Miracles* teacher, was not experiencing miracles in his own life. His income fluctuated constantly between feast and famine. He had grown up in relative ease and was given quite a bit of money from his family, which he continued to spend until there was none left.

His father, a very successful and emotionally unavailable man, had had an affair while on a business trip, which caused the family to disintegrate. His mother, who depended on Jared to now "be the man," constantly blamed his father's success as the cause of his affair, with an addendum that men can't be trusted. In other words, financial success causes infidelity.

Jared realized that he had made an unconscious decision not to be financially successful as a way to stay in relationship with his mother and make sure he would not replicate his father's actions. He began to see that his parents' marriage was not so black and white as he'd originally believed. As he gathered new stories of financially successful men who were also trustworthy in their relationships, he created a new reality for himself. He took responsibility for his collusion with his mother to hold himself back and wrote a different story for himself. As a result, his new empowering paradigm became "I am a man of integrity. I generously bring my gifts, wisdom and talents to the world. I invite money to flow and dance with me as my friend."

While our world can conspire to wound us, we are greater than our wounds. We come into this world knowing we are enough, that we are loveable and deserving of love. But, if those who are supposed to love us hurt us instead, we often decide it must be our fault or we are flawed. The state of childhood can be a very powerless state and it is easy to forget that our essential self is whole and complete and we are enough.

My dear friend, Joe, has grappled with feeling unworthy, unlovable, and not enough all his life. Even though his essence radiates love to others, he's struggled to love himself. His father was extremely critical of him as a child, giving him the message that he was flawed. Staying in relationship with his father required him to continue to hold the story that he was not enough, which manifested in underearning. Financial struggle has been a constant source of shame and pain for Joe. His big "ah ha" was the realization that as a child he'd concluded: "I need to be loved by my father. If he thinks I am not enough, in order to be loved by him, I need to think the same about myself."

The unconscious decisions we make as children continue to be reinforced. In Joe's case, his father's critical voice had transmuted into his own critical voice, continuing to tell him all the ways he was a "f**k up." In a sense, his father cursed him by giving him constant messages of inadequacy. Joe's own messages continued to reinforce them.

For Joe, understanding how his money issues were a direct reflection of his unhealed relationship with his father opened a door to transforming his relationship with himself and money. He had an almost miraculous experience of being bathed in a healing loving light that felt divine. The light began to permeate his entire being, supporting him to release the core sense of shame and self-judgment he'd held for so many years. This allowed Joe to write a new story in which his father was supportive and loving, resulting in greater confidence, self-love and not surprisingly, more money.

Understanding that in the unconscious mind there is no time helps to explain why our stories, memories and the resulting decisions we make regarding "truth" remain stuck. But the most amazing thing is that, since the unconscious mind doesn't live in current time and space, rewriting the story with new conclusions and endings pretty much switches the old files with new ones. The story I shared earlier in the chapter about my inner children now living in a home for children that's safe and enriching is an example of the healing power of creating new narratives. This "new reality" has slowly rippled into all areas of my adult life, bringing a "new normal" of hope, resilience, peace and joy.

In her childhood, Carly's father would sit with her brother and walk him through the *Wall Street Journal,* coaching him on the principles of money and investment. Curious, Carly begged her father to let her sit in on their conversations. His response was "You're a girl, you don't need to learn about money."

She shared, "The belief I came away with was girls have less value and don't need to learn about money. Sadly, I carried that into my adult life. I have consistently struggled with my relationship with money, while my brother is incredibly rich. It's not fair and I blame my father."

In her new narrative, Carly had a seat at the table along with her brother. Her father lovingly taught her how to understand money and wise investing. He praised her questions and curiosity. He gave her the message that she was important and had the ability to create wealth in all areas of her life. She felt seen and celebrated for her gifts. Her new empowering paradigm became: "Girls are important and just as smart as boys, including their of understanding money and wealth."

A common childhood wound is to be shamed for asking for something. One of my clients shared with me that when she would ask her father for lunch money he would painfully gather his change and shame her, saying, "Do you think I'm made of money?" In my own childhood, I came to the conclusion that I should not ask for anything, because I wasn't going to get it anyway. The problem with this is that asking clearly is the key to manifesting. Asking for a raise, asking to be paid for a service or a product, all of these abilities are essential for Money to be able to dance with us.

Being able to rewrite our story gives us back a sense of power in our lives. It won't change what actually happened in the "real world." But, since the unconscious mind doesn't distinguish between "real" or imagined, it doesn't matter. Changing our narratives creates new perceptions which opens the door to new options.

A few years ago, I was listening to an interview with a man who stepped off a curb and was hit by a car, leaving him a quadriplegic. He shared that the bitterness and anger he felt after the accident was all-encompassing. As a result, he began to descend into despair, dramatically undermining his healing.

One of his therapists suggested that he write a different story. In the new story he didn't step off the curb, the accident never happened, and life went on as before. Amazingly, even though his situation was the same, playing out a different story helped him to release the bitterness and anger, to find meaning in the experience he was living, and to envision a future that was filled with possibility. Since the stories we tell ourselves create our reality, rewriting our stories brings new information into our internal system and a new sense of possibility.

The Wisdom of Our Wounds - Healed People Heal

Years ago, I was taking a workshop where we were instructed to draw a line down the paper. On one side, we wrote down all of the trauma we'd experienced in our lives. On the other side, we wrote down all the experiences that gave us the wisdom and insight we needed to be effective as a healer and psychotherapist. Amazingly, the same things on the trauma side were on the wisdom side. I hadn't realized that there was a gift in those experiences. It wasn't until that moment that I was able to see the connection so clearly.

A profound transformational thought leader and marketing coach, Jeffrey Van Dyk,[7] believes that our early wounds, when healed, are the sign posts for our work in the world. They become the exquisite and unique constellation of wisdom that we bring to our interactions and environments.

Rewriting our childhood money stories is a gift we give to ourselves. As we heal, we empower others to heal.

---

7   www.jeffreyvandyk.com/

Dance Steps

Pick one story that you hold from your childhood that's affecting your relationship with money or what is possible. Write a new story with a different outcome, where you received the resources you needed at the time, where you heard what you needed to hear, where it was the way you would have wanted it. Write in whatever way feels right—either in the first person, in the third person, or by creating a story of a child with your name.

Just as my own inner children are happily hanging out in a loving "Home for Children," your own inner children can begin to create a new reality by choosing what they would have wanted instead.

Having rewritten the story, create a new empowering paradigm that will align with this new reality. Write it in the present tense. Use words that invoke a feeling of excitement and possibility. I like to write my empowering paradigms on 3x5 cards, carry them with me, and read them daily.

CHAPTER 6

Forgiveness Brings Freedom

"The practice of forgiveness is our most important contribution to the healing of the world."

Marianne Williamson

"Forgiveness is not an occasional act, it is a constant attitude."

Martin Luther King

We've now explored the stories of money, the collective, our ancestors and our childhood. It's true that healing all of these wounds can be life changing. But what about those adult situations that didn't end well, where money figured prominently? Unfortunately, money often becomes imprinted with the anger, hurt, or shame we felt in ourselves or for the person who harmed us in some way.

Being Hostage to Past Money Trauma

"I hate money." I was surprised at the intensity of the statement that came from the petite woman sitting across the dinner table from me when I shared I was writing a book on money.

Curious, I asked her why she had such strong feelings towards money. She began to tell me that she was supposed to receive a large settlement from her divorce. Unfortunately, before she received it, she had agreed to let her ex-husband invest the money in a deal that went bust. She looked at me with a mixture of rage and sadness and said, "That money was supposed to be for my retirement. Now, I have nothing to retire with."

I asked, "But, why is that money's fault?"

Her answer was, "Well, I guess it's not really money's fault, but I hate money just the same." Unfortunately, even though it wasn't money's fault, money was still the one holding the blame.

Few of us are immune from making investments that later turned out to bad. I've invested twice in a pyramid scheme that I wasn't aware I was investing in. I'd trusted friends who convinced me it was legitimate. Losing the money brought feelings of anger, stupidity, shame and betrayal.

My friend Mary loaned her former boyfriend a lot of money to start a business that was never successful. After they broke up, she held so much shame it took her a long time to even talk about the lost funds, much less take action to reclaim them. She finally went to an attorney and ultimately to court. She happily began to receive the court ordered payments, only to get a notice a few months later that the ex was filing for bankruptcy. She was told by her attorney not to bother trying to get any more money and just to be grateful for what she'd already gotten.

There are numerous ways to become traumatized around money. Joanne started a business that failed. A number of factors resulted in its failure, including the fact that her accountant was stealing from her. She didn't know enough to understand why the numbers weren't working out. As a result, she had to file for bankruptcy. Instead of seeing how much courage it took to start a business, she was stuck in shame and guilt, which kept her hostage and afraid to try again. Joanne wasn't aware of the fact that many successful entrepreneurs fail numerous times before they become successful.

Where is money still stuck in unpleasant memories or stories of being a victim? Did you work in a place where the working conditions were really poor, but you stayed because you didn't think you had any options? Were you fired from a job? Were you put in a position that was above your ability and you felt like an imposter trying to pretend you knew what you were doing? Did you have a boss that treated you unfairly or was abusive? Did you lose a lot of money because you trusted someone, loaning them money, and they never paid it back? Did you allow someone to use you financially because you were afraid they would leave you or because you wanted their love? Did you stay in a relationship or situation that was abusive out of fear of financial instability? Or did you stay in a loveless marriage for the same reason?

Debt, for many, is a huge source of shame and burden. It's important to realize that you are not your debt. You are not a bad person. One of my clients was stuck in shame because he'd gone through a financial crisis in his business and spent all of his retirement. His self-talk was "I can't be trusted with money," which he continued to replay in his life. Bringing compassion to the situation brought healing and forgiveness. As a result, he was able to unburden the parts of him that held shame and blame and move on.

These money-related memories locked in shame, guilt, fear, anger, betrayal, sadness, loss, etc. keep both money and ourselves hostage. Having cleared ancestral and childhood traumas, healing these last remnants is one of the final frontiers.

Freeing Yourself with Forgiveness

Forgiveness had always felt like one of those things that you do because it's supposed to be good for you, not necessarily because you like it. To me, it was sort of like kale, which I very much dislike, but has become

Gale West, MA, MFA

one of the latest "good for you" foods in the western world that seem to dominate way too many menus for my taste.

But, I've realized that forgiveness is a gift we give to our selves. All of these stuck emotions continue to bind us to the people and situations that created them. We were harmed by another, we harmed another, or we harmed ourselves. In our painful money stories, because money is a major player, it becomes locked into the hurt. As a result, our relationship with money is tainted with the emotional pain still stuck there. Our anger and sense of violation gets unjustly projected onto money. Is it money's fault that Bernie Madoff stole a lot of people's money? Or that an accountant embezzled? Or that an old boyfriend didn't pay back his loan?

Forgiving does not justify the actions of the perpetrator. It just clears the emotional ties that bind us.

Our stuck feelings keep us stuck.

Without emotional freedom, we're limited in what we can create in our lives. Anything that feels remotely similar will reactivate all the negative feelings associated with it. We moderate our choices in order to ensure "it won't happen again." Thus, life gets constricted and our options become limited. Forgiveness opens the door.

Forgiving doesn't mean we forget, but it says, "I have the ability to learn from the experiences in my life and have compassion for myself as either a victim or a victimizer. I choose to be free." If healing and transforming our relationship with money is a sacred journey, then opening ourselves to forgiveness is a gift to our soul.

Dance Steps

If you think back on your life, where are places that your relationship with money might be stuck in a story, memory or incident? Who do you need to forgive, including yourself? Are there institutions, organizations, companies, leaders, or groups that you also want to put on your forgiveness list?

The following are powerful forgiveness prayers to support your forgiveness practice.

Consider saying one of them daily for the next 30 days. Your intention to forgive and to be free will support the process.

If other memories emerge over the next month, add them to your list.

Forgiveness Prayer

(to be said three times in a row)

As you are reciting the forgiveness prayer, imagine all the stories, memories, and connections being bathed in light and all energetic ties being cut and released.

I now choose to forgive and release any harm done, consciously or unconsciously, to me by another; any harm I may have done, consciously or unconsciously, to another; and any harm I may have done, consciously or unconsciously, to myself, particularly in regard to money.

I ask that I now be released from all non-beneficial energetic ties to the stories, memories, or people. I ask for healing and blessings for all concerned. Thank you. Amen

Ho'oponopono

Another powerful forgiveness prayer is Ho'oponopono, a traditional Hawaiian practice of forgiveness and reconciliation. Ho'oponopono means "to make right." I say it daily to bring re-alignment from any way I've been out of alignment with myself or another.

It is simply, *"I'm sorry. Please forgive me. Thank you. I love you."*

When I say it, I say it on behalf of all concerned. This includes me, the other, and all the circumstances.

It doesn't matter which prayer you use. Pick the one that feels right for you. It is a gift you give yourself—the gift of freedom!

Dancing with Money

CHAPTER 7

Money as Guide and Friend

*"For the triumph of good, we have to make a choice. We can
enlist on the side of good by prospering, making money and
using our wealth to help others."*

Rohinton Mistry

The idea of guidance and support from the "invisible world"
permeates all spiritual traditions, whether it be angels, ancestors,
the Holy Spirit, Higher Power, or animal guides. Included in the
acknowledgement of spiritual guidance, but not associated with a
spiritual tradition, is the cutting-edge psychotherapeutic modality I've
referenced in earlier chapters, Internal Family Systems. Since money
is intricately tied to navigating effectively in life, guidance and support
from the "invisible world" could be a helpful thing.

In my many years of communicating with Money as a consciousness, I
have come to understand its many aspects. There is the Divine essence
of Money. This is a very high vibration that is intimately connected to
Divine Source. There is Money, which is the consciousness that still
holds all the pain, suffering and sorrow we've projected on it. This is
the money that is still stuck in the outhouse. Then there is our personal
connection to Money as guide. This is connected to, but separate from
the pure consciousness of Money. Your Money guide is unique to you. It
has a deep understanding of the role of money in our third dimensional
world and is assigned to support you on your human journey, so you,
money, and your Money Guide all dance together.

By having a personal relationship with Money, you will discover a loving being that is delighted to support you to create a joyous and fulfilling life. As your friend, it is intimately aware of the stress of financial struggle. It knows that feelings of lack and "not enough" are a cause of great suffering. Money aches for your peace of mind, wants to hold you in comfort and invite you into the experience of enough. As a spiritual being having a human experience, your ability to develop a deep and abiding relationship with Money as Divine Source will ensure a greater sense of ease in your human journey.

Money's loving support will help you to heal deep wounds you may be holding about yourself, your worth, or value. Your relationship to things and consumption will change. Your trust in yourself and the Divine will grow. If you used money as a way to feel better about yourself, or blamed money for feeling trapped in a job or relationship, you will find a newfound sense of freedom. This profound relationship with Money will open you to new possibilities, including an increasing sense of generosity with yourself and others.

I am often asked if people's Money guides are actually angels. I have no idea. But, angel or not, Money will appear in the form that is perfect for you. As an angel, an animal spirit, a dragon, a rainbow, or just the felt sense of a wise being—these are some of the various forms in which Money as guide has appeared to people. In my many years of working with people, I have come to *know* that we all have guides, be they angels or wise beings. Whether we are aware of them or not, they are available and will happily show up to support us if we ask. Since this is the plane of free will, they cannot interfere with our choices even though they ache to be of service. We must invite them in. Money is ready for your invitation!

Money As Guide

In my initial communication with Money, I sensed a very kind, loving male presence. That connection was a powerful impetus, not only for my own healing, but also to support the healing of many others. As my relationship with Money has grown and changed, Money now appears as a large prancing horse. "Get on up. I'll take you where you need to go." It was Money's joke on me since I often tell people to ride the horse of life instead of being the horse.

A devout Catholic, my friend Tom's personal Money connection is represented as the Holy Spirit. At first it seemed a little strange to him that the Holy Spirit would also represent Money's divine essence. But over time, he realized that Money and spirituality were not as mutually exclusive as he had thought. Quite the contrary. The Holy Spirit helped him to see that when more spiritual people have good relationships with money, the better the world will be.

As mentioned earlier, Money as guide, has appeared to people in many creative forms, including a huge purple bow, a dance, a ball of light, a green cartoon Betty Boop, an angel, the Statue of Liberty, a huge winged Mercury, and a Sammy Davis Junior look-a-like with a gold lamé suit. One of my favorites is a pink dragon named Porsche. The common characteristic of all of them is a loving, kind, supportive presence.

Brandon, a very powerful healer, had a very tenuous relationship with money. In his own words, he describes his experience of connecting with his Money guide:

Guided inward to know my Money guide, I saw myself scrounging around on the ground in the hard scrabble, trying to find sustenance on my hands and knees. It was hard and painful. Then I saw a horse standing right next to me. My Money guide! I could ride with him wherever I wanted to go, and I could have this experience all the time! There was nothing threatening or scary about him—he just wanted to help and support me in what I wanted to do! I cried tears of relief as I saw the truth of the message that was being given to me—it didn't have to be so hard! Riding with him, I felt an amazing sense of freedom, the wind whipping by my ears and through my hair as we headed for new adventures and greener pastures!

He went on to say, *"Since then, I've begun to spend a few minutes or more each day with him. He turned pink, and then grew wings to be this amazing Pegasus! His name was Clyde, which made me laugh so hard! We feel a deep joy and affection for one another. I feel safer and more secure in my business than ever before. I feel so blessed and abundant!"*

Here is Julia's experience of her new connection to Money as guide.

I used to be fearful of money—for many years I didn't respect it, and always worried about not having enough. I connected with the spirit of money. It was definitely female. It told me that it wanted to be respected, appreciated, used, enjoyed and shared. Since the workshop, I've experienced evidence of abundance—in financial and many other ways. I still have occasional moments of panic, but mostly, I feel calm, confident and joyful about my relationship with Money. We're friends now!

Money can show up in many ways, not just more money in the bank. The following is my own example of Money's wonderful support. While exiting the plane, after sitting for an uncomfortable 16-hour trip to Hong Kong, I walked past business first class. The pillows looked fluffier, the blankets nicer and there were little pods enabling one to lie down flat and sleep. With conviction I declared, "The next time I come here I want to travel like this." Amazingly, my wish was granted! Six months later, while booking tickets to Hong Kong to teach a money retreat, a window popped up on the website. "For an extra $200, would you like to travel business first class?" Oh, yes! As a result, I paid only $1200 for tickets worth $4200.

Stretching out in my comfortable business class pod, my partner and I looked at each other and said, "Thank you, Money!" The pillows were indeed fluffier, the blankets nicer, the food better, and the wine was excellent. We arrived rested, as opposed to exhausted like in the past.

While in Hong Kong, Money gifted us again. The apartment we'd originally booked was uninhabitable and in an undesirable location. We were able to get a refund on the original space and ended up in a lovely apartment in a vibrant and highly convenient part of Hong Kong.

There are numerous other stories of Money gifting my life and those I've worked with after creating a deep and lasting relationship with their Money guides. This is just one benefit of Divine Source, as your Money guide, showing up to bring more ease, flow and grace. Here is Kay's experience. *"My energy and attitudes around money have transformed. I feel relaxed and confident. I'm peacefully assertive with my clients about standing firm in my value, and my business revenue has grown substantially without me needing to push hard. I wanted to be friends with Money. And now I am."*

Once you connect with Money, recognize that your relationship needs to be nurtured and attended to. Your life will change as you show up with openness and constancy. Money as guide is always available to support you. You just need to show up. It's an act of faith, both in yourself and in the Divine. Your new relationship with Money as guide will grow with attention and constancy. Money loves attention! In return, you'll begin to experience wonderful synchronicities. Opportunities will appear. People will gift you. You may find what you are looking for on sale or at amazing prices, such as my Hong Kong example. You'll have a sense of freedom and trust, and begin to lean into the knowing that you are enough, there is enough, and there will always be more than enough.

In many ways, our connection to money isn't about money, but *about our relationship with ourselves and what is possible.* Money will help you heal any "not good enough" parts, any distrusting parts; it will help you to open your receiving channels, to connect you with desire; and it will help you to know that you will always be cared for. Remember, Money as guide is a representative for Divine Source. Paradoxically, they are separate, but also the same.

Starting a Dialogue

The following visualization is designed to connect you with your own Money guide. Remember that Money will come in the form that is perfect for you. You may see an image or just have a felt sense of a being. Don't worry if nothing comes, just send love from you heart and invite Money to come dance with you.

If you wrote a letter to Money, the exercise from chapter one, then you've already begun the process. If so, revisit your initial communication with Money. Take some time to consider what, if anything, has changed as you've "danced" through the book this far. Congratulate and honor the journey you've been traveling.

Dancing with Money Meditation

There are four aspects to this meditation: gratitude for what you already have, taking responsibility for the relationship with money you've had in the past, helping money to heal, and the last—inviting your Money guide to come forward and beginning communication with it. You may want to have someone read this visualization or record it. Or go to moneycomedancewithme.com for a free recording of this meditation.

Take a deep breath and close your eyes. Take another deep breath, hold it for a few seconds and exhale. Take another deep breath and as you exhale; let the tension in your body move out with your breath. Take a deep breath and imagine a big wave of relaxation moving over your whole body. Take another deep breath and imagine another big wave of relaxation moving over your whole body.

Now, feel the clothing you are wearing against your skin. Imagine all the people who helped to make these clothes. The designer, those who worked in the factory that made the cloth, that dyed the cloth, that cut it, sewed it, packed it, transported it, displayed it, sold it. All of these people brought their divinity to the marketplace. Thank money and all of the people that your money touched so that you could be wearing these clothes on your body.

Imagine the home you're living in. Many people brought their divinity to the marketplace to allow you to have a home for yourself and those who share it with you. The builder, carpenter, those that cut the wood and transported the wood, the tiles in your bathroom, and the numerous fixtures in your home. Thank money and all the people your money touched. Now, look around your home at the things you love, that make your home comfortable and beautiful. Many people brought their divinity to the marketplace to create these things. Thank money and all the people your money touched.

Now imagine the food in your kitchen. Consider all the people around the world who helped to grow it, pick it, pack or can it, transport it, and all the others who helped to bring this food to your kitchen. They too brought their divinity to the marketplace. Again, thank money and all the people your money touched.

Now, take a few moments and allow yourself to apologize to money for any way you blamed it for your troubles, or thought of it as bad, any way you didn't respect it, or care for it, or attend to it. For any way you might have wasted it, or held shame around it.

Now imagine that you are standing under a waterfall of light in whatever color that would be healing and cleansing. Feel the light flowing over your whole being, clearing all the negative feelings you may be still holding around money or yourself in relationship to money.

Now imagine that the light is turning a beautiful gold. Feel that you are being infused with golden light. Invite money to join you. As you do, imagine that both you and money are being healed. Imagine that the golden light is helping money to wash away all pain, suffering, and sorrow that has been projected upon it so it can be freed to be an agent for good. So that it can be an agent for Divine Love in the marketplace.

As you stand under that waterfall, imagine that your Money guide is standing next to you. As you connect with it, you can feel its presence growing stronger. Is there an image? A feeling? A sound? In what way is your Money guide presenting itself to you? Invite it to dance with you in your life.

Once you have connected with your Money guide, begin to dialogue with it. Ask your guide, "What message do you have for me?" "How can we dance together?" "How do I deepen my relationship with you?"

When you're ready, thank Money for coming to you. Take a deep breath and return to normal consciousness.

Dance Steps

After you've created a connection with your Money guide, it's important to grow the relationship. Here are some ideas that have worked both for me and others.

- *Meditate together. Set an intention for the meditation. Document your insights.*
- *Imagine your Money guide in front of you. Send it your love and blessings. Feel the same energy coming back.*
- *Invite your Money guide to dance with you. Imagine that you are dancing together.*
- *Thank the goodness that Money brings to you throughout the day.*
- *Dialogue with your Money guide. Connect. Bring your concerns, joys and delights. Listen for the response.*
- *The following are suggestions to help your dialogue:*
  1. *Access your Money guide through dominant, non-dominant hand writing. You are the dominant hand, and your Money guide talks back through your non-dominant hand. Employing the non-dominant hand for your Money guide immediately connects you to your intuitive brain.[8]*
  2. *Active Imagination is a technique that's a little easier than dominant, non-dominant hand writing. You just dialogue by drawing a line down the middle of the page. You are on the left side and Money answers on the right. Or by taking turns down the page. Identify who is speaking during your conversation. You — Money*

---

8   *The Power of Your Other Hand* by Lucia Capacchioni, goes into depth regarding dominant, non-dominant hand communication. I highly recommend it.

CHAPTER 8

Leaning into Trust

"Trust is the glue of life. It is the most essential ingredient in effective communication. It's the foundational principle that holds all relationships."

Stephen Covey

"Trust: A firm belief in the reliability, truth, ability, or strength of someone or something."

Webster's Dictionary

" Trust is a big issue for me. When I have money, I don't trust that I'll be able to hold onto it or spend it wisely. When I don't have it, I don't trust that it will come again. It will be hard to get it back, or it will be less." This was my friend Kelly's response in a conversation that explored how trust and money are deeply connected.

Trust and money are ultimately tied to issues around safety, belonging, value and deserving. The questions it triggers are: Can I trust money to show up? Can I trust myself to show up? Can I trust that there is a benevolent universe that gives a sh*t about me? (For most people that translates to God or whatever name you want to give to the Divine Creator.)

There is a direct correlation in being able to trust Money, ourselves, and Divine Source to show up. Our unconscious mind does not distinguish between any of them. It's pretty much all the same theme that gets played out—specifically, "I can't trust that I will get what I need."

Having established a personal relationship connection with Money as a guide and friend in the last chapter, addressing any lurking issues of trust parts of you may have is essential. Otherwise these doubts will sabotage your ability to grow and deepen that relationship.

Trusting Source

Money and trust in a benevolent universe are intimately linked. For those of us who've had our trust violated in some way, the idea of being able to "let go and let God" sounds good, but in reality isn't so easy to do. From my own life, money trauma, God trauma, and childhood trauma converged to create huge trust issues that resulted in believing I was all alone in the universe. The ironic thing was that I didn't believe it was true for others, only for me. As a result, as much as I ached to trust, for many parts of me, it was the equivalent of a free fall out of an airplane without a parachute.

In my own work with Money, this was one of the critical things I needed to address in order for my own transformation to occur, both in regards to money, and my relationship with Divine Source.

So, how does one regain trust once it's been lost? For me, it was to practice "leaning into trust." In other words, opening the door to a new possibility. I wasn't requiring my untrusting parts to believe anything. I was inviting them to be open to suspending disbelief that it is safe to trust and the universe actually does have my back. Since trust is earned, maybe if I opened the door to new data I would actually find it. At the end of each day, I documented all of its magical synchronicities. I thanked both Money and the universe when I felt supported. Over time, the growing evidence of a different reality began to emerge. With that, little by little, a new reality of trust ensued and ultimately co-creation with Divine Source.

Nina is a wonderful example of addressing trust issues head on. A tall, beautiful woman with straight blond hair, she approached me at a conference we were both attending. "When I listened to the money meditation on your website, my Money Guide appeared as an incredibly loving feminine being. Her message to me was, "Why do you worry so much? I will always be there for you."

With fear and sadness in her eyes, Nina continued, "It was such an amazingly profound experience that I was afraid that it would never happen again, so I just shut down."

I gave her a big hug and gently said, "Trust is earned. Give Money a chance to earn your trust. I truly believe she is willing, if you are willing."

Nina's email arrived a few months later. "I decided to allow Money to earn my trust. She (my Money Guide) continues to be an angel in my life. When I focus only on how she evades me and resentment towards those I feel have kept her away, my life becomes smaller and I feel pinched off from her Grace. When I trust that she supports money to flow to me like the breath that's always available and I breathe in deeply, I feel calm, appreciative, devotional of her... and whole."

I was struck by the beauty and profundity of Nina's message. It took courage for Nina to lean into trust. As a result, the previously traumatized parts of her, whose trust had been violated, were given evidence of a new reality. A door that had been previously closed was now open.

Trusting Ourselves

While being able to trust Money and the Universe to show up is key, being able to trust ourselves to also show up is the equivalent to turning the key. Many of us make commitments to ourselves that we consistently break. The result is a relationship with ourselves that is tentative, at best. This lack of inner integrity sends a powerful message that we are undependable and not trustworthy. It produces shame and lots of critical voices beating us up.

Showing up for money, attending to it, saving it and spending it wisely are all ways that we show up for ourselves. But if that relationship is fraught with feelings of fear and lack of worth, it is difficult to consistently make it happen. Money loves commitment and intention. For it to show up for us, we need to show up for it. Money reflects back to us how we are with it. Thus, if we aren't consistent, it won't be consistent back.

Change Starts with a Choice

My friend, Tom, had always struggled with his relationship with money. As much he ached to grow his savings, he would unfailingly dip into his account when things got tight. He began to see how his lack of trust in himself was eroding his relationship with himself and money. He also saw how it was contributing to his money situation yo-yoing from highs to lows. Wanting something different, he knew that the only way to make it happen would be to consistently show up in a new way.

He decided to start small. He committed to saving at least $20 a week. He opened an account in a bank that was not connected to any of his other accounts so it wouldn't be easy to transfer money. Each week he honored his commitment. Walking the mile and a half to the bank became a ritual that increased his sense of self-trust and confidence.

One week, all he had was a twenty-dollar bill. His regular account was overdrawn. He was tempted to take the money out of savings to cover it as he had always done in the past. But, instead, he walked the mile and a half to the bank and deposited the $20. To him, that was the turning point—the beginning of a new relationship with money and himself.

In his own words, "As I was walking to the bank I began to feel something change inside. I was no longer the failure I'd always told myself I was. I knew that, from this day forward, I was not only committed to be someone who saves. I was committing to me. I was someone who showed up for me, for my self-worth, for my success, and for my life."

As a result, with his new trust in himself to show up for money, Money and the universe responded in magical ways. Over time, Tom began to experience the financial ease and stability he had only dreamed possible. The last I spoke with him he smiled saying, "My business is where I've always wanted it to be. I am happier and more successful than ever. I continue to save regularly and know that I will always have more than enough."

Leaning into Trust

Once our trust has been eroded, it's not going to magically come back without some new evidence. Psychologist John Gottman has done some of the most definitive research on intimate relationships. He talks about the importance of deposits in the emotional bank. These are small, loving actions that help one build up resilience and trust in relationships. Since our relationships with Money, ourselves, and the Divine are actually very intimate, deposits in the emotional trust bank are key to building trust.

Our brain naturally notices what isn't working and often doesn't notice all the little ways things *are* working. By documenting daily how Money, the Universe, or you showed up for yourself, you begin the process of putting deposits into the trust bank. It won't happen overnight, but being willing to "lean into trust" will give the parts of you whose trust was eroded evidence that it may be safe to trust again.

Previously afraid to trust, Nina made the decision to move beyond her fear and lean into trust. It took courage due to the pain of old trauma and disappointment. Her Money guide did return, and was just as loving as the first time. As the relationship continued to grow, Nina opened the door wider, and there was more trust, and more deposits accrued in the trust bank on both sides. In her own words, "It has been a truly deep and transformational journey for me."

For Tom, learning that he could trust himself to show up for Money (and himself) rippled out into numerous areas of his life. It didn't happen overnight. Shifts and changes happened over time. He had to be able to forgive himself for mistakes of the past and choose to open the door to a new reality. He recognized that he was stuck in an old pattern and identity that wasn't serving him anymore. His weekly walk to the bank became the baby steps that created a "new normal."

It's a process. When we've lost trust, it takes a while to get it back. It begins by noticing the little shifts and changes. These include the ways you show up for yourself and for Money, and how Money and the Universe shows up for you. Consistently acknowledging the deposits that were made in your trust bank will be a deep, profound and life changing journey.

Dance Steps

Since trust is earned, it's important to acknowledge the ways you, Money and the universe show up to earn that trust. These can be actions taken, connections made, synchronicities, moments of joy, awe, or anything else that feels appropriate as deposits made in the trust account. I recommend taking a few minutes at the end of the day documenting any or all deposits made in the trust bank. This will begin the process of healing eroded trust and establishing a powerful profound relationship with your Money guide.

Since consistency is key to creating trust, the more you regularly connect and communicate with your Money Guide, the greater your trust in yourself and Money will grow. Consider asking Money for further guidance on issues of trust that may need healing.

Our trust is eroded because of some sort of hurt, trauma or disappointment. As a result, in addition to working on leaning into trust, revisiting the forgiveness chapter would be helpful. Forgiving yourself, Money and/or God, using the forgiveness prayer or Ho'oponopono, will help to release any unresolved hurt, blame or shame. This will further assist you to open the door to trust.

CHAPTER 9

Creating a Money Relationship Vision

"One's vision is not a road map but a compass."

Peter Block

"In order to carry a positive action,
we must develop here a positive vision."

Dalai Lama

The Power of Vision

During my time as a psychotherapist, I frequently worked with couples. I liken people's relationships to gardens. In the beginning, they would consistently plant their garden with beautiful flowering memories and loving actions. Over time, too many couples forget to water, weed, or tend the garden until it's overgrown, filled with weeds, or almost dead.

Instead of focusing on what wasn't working, which they knew all too well, I would start by inviting couples to dream again. What would it look like if their relationship was a ten? In their visioning, I would ask them to include what was still good in the relationship, in addition to what was needed for it to be the best they could imagine.

As we worked together, each person brought different nuances of what was important to them individually and collectively. The result was a vision statement they both agreed upon that expressed everything they required to have a phenomenally fabulous relationship. Thereafter, I would begin each session by revisiting their relationship vision and invite them to acknowledge any little shifts or movement towards that vision. (Building trust in the bank.) Amazingly, qualities that seemed impossible would magically begin to appear. This is the power of vision.

Since Money is one of the most intimate relationships you will ever have, would you not also want a phenomenally powerful and fabulous vision statement for that relationship? Even though it may be difficult to consider, friends and spouses may come and go. But unless you are mentally incapacitated and unable to financially care for yourself, Money will *always* be in your life.

In the past, your relationship with Money was influenced by your family stories, the institutions you grew up with, your own stories, and the attitude of the culture in which you lived. As a result, the garden of your relationship with Money was mostly planted by someone or something else. In the earlier chapters of this book, we explored all the different money traumas that might have gotten planted there. Hopefully, you've taken the time do some weeding and healing. Now you get to choose the type of relationship you want to have instead. No longer bound by the past, having an intentional relationship with Money is something you get to create on your own terms. Taking the time to create a vision of the kind of relationship you want will more than likely ensure that you will make it happen.

Your commitment to have an intentional and conscious relationship with Money is about your commitment to yourself. You get to plant the kind of relationship garden you want, one that you are willing to lovingly tend. Fill it with the flowers of expansion, growth, value, worth and delight. Know that Money aches to express itself through you as an extension of the value you bring to the marketplace.

Having a clear Money relationship vision is a gift that will sustain you and your relationship with Money for a long time. You will experience incredible results and a powerful connection that will last you throughout your life inviting flow, respect, commitment, and clarity. Generously give yourself the time to explore what an amazing relationship with Money would look like. If you show up for Money, it will happily show up for you in exchange.

Creating Your Money Relationship Vision

If you wrote a letter to Money in the first chapter, revisit it. How has your relationship changed as you've danced thus far with this book? Take time to celebrate yourself, any shifts you notice, and your commitment to having a powerful, deep and loving relationship with Money. Acknowledging and praising any big or small shifts or transformations is key to creating more.

Consider these questions:

- *What qualities would be present?*
- *How do you want to use your money to have a greater impact in the world?*
- *How will you honor money?*
- *How will you treat it?*
- *How will you help it to flow to you?*
- *How do you want it to treat you?*
- *How will you help it to grow and flourish?*

Once you've explored these questions on your own, begin to dialogue with Money. Create your relationship vision together. Give yourself the gift of thought, time, attention and intention. Create a vision powerful enough that your heart sings as you read it, one that pulls you towards its manifestation. A powerful vision means you are committed to furthering trust in yourself, the universe and Money.

My Money Relationship Vision

Here is my Money relationship vision. You may borrow any or all of it, if you so choose.

Dear Money,

Come dance with me. May it be a dance of delight, joy, peace, ease and grace.

As we dance together, I trust that you will always be there for me and I commit to respect, attend and care for you wisely in return.

Guide me, so together we may grow and flourish, be it through the divine expression of my gifts in the marketplace, savings, investments, or any other ways you want to dance with me, bringing financial independence, ease, and grace.

I commit to spend you wisely, consciously, and from a place of enough, so you can be an agent for good in the world.

I commit to being generous with myself, those I love, and those causes I feel passionate about so you may happily flow.

Let us dance together. Bless me as I bless you. Thank you.

Don't be afraid to ask for what you really want! Consider sharing your vision with someone you know and trust. They can help you get beyond habitual beliefs about what you can have and ask for.

Dance Steps

Create your own intentional money mission statement. Give yourself permission to tweak until it feels "right." A really powerful intention statement will feel exciting and point to a new empowering paradigm. Does it make your heart sing when you read it? If so, then you've succeeded.

As in any intention statement, it works if you work it. So, read it daily. Consider adding your daily successes in regards to your intentional relationship with Money, along with the last chapter's suggestion to consistently document deposits in the trust bank.

Allow for your intention statement to be a work in progress. As your relationship with Money and yourself grows and transforms, your intention statement may also. Continue to dialogue with Money to expand and deepen your relationship.

Dancing with Conscious Co-Creation

CHAPTER 10

"The Transceiver"

"The best way to predict your future is to create it."

Peter Drucker

In one of my early communications with Money I heard:

"You must become aware of your transceiver. All of creation is constantly sending and receiving. But, most humans are not conscious that they create their lives in each moment by what they are sending and what they are able to receive. You must become aware of what you are sending and receiving. This is the key to true power."

The idea of a transceiver was new to me. I'd never heard of a transceiver. I thought I'd received a cool new word from the Universe. Months later, while sharing the quote with my partner, he perked up. "A transceiver is a real thing. It's not something that Money made up. It's a ham radio term. A transceiver is a device that has the ability to both transmit and receive signals on the same frequency. If your transceiver is misaligned, you could be asking for something on one frequency, and not realize it's showing up on another."

I've read and reread this quote from Money, and every time I do, I am humbled by what it implies; that true power lies in *absolute clarity* that what you are sending into the field is what you truly desire and in your ability to receive it when it comes.

Unfortunately, most of us spend our time hanging out in the past or the future, having anxiety over what happened or worrying about what will happen. Since we're constantly creating in each moment with what we're sending and receiving, reconnecting to our divinity as the creators of our lives requires mindfulness and awareness. The process is a continual dance with our level of understanding and connection to inner knowing and our soul's path. In other words, moment by moment we must consciously choose aligning or realigning the clarity of our signals in response to what the outer world is reflecting back to us.

There are four aspects to the creation cycle, all of which are intrinsically connected to the signals you're sending into the field. Desire, action, receiving, and completion. If there is a barrier to any of these, your transceiver's signals will be muddy and your ability to live in alignment with what delights your soul will be limited.

If there's a barrier to desire, and you have no idea what you want, you'll never know if you actually got it, or not. This creates a life of frustration and an aching heart, because deep down inside, some part of you actually *does* know what you want, but something is blocking you from consciously knowing.

You may know what you want, but if you have a barrier to action, there is no movement toward making it happen. Since we live in a three-dimensional world of form and substance, our interactions with the world are what brings our desires to us. Taking action, seizing opportunities, and saying Yes! are the signals that tell the Universe, "I am committed." A strong desire or clarity in sending signals will bring the opportunities and synchronicities. But without taking action when they appear, one stays in the plane of "wishing" instead of manifesting.

Years ago, I became obsessed with a desire to travel to Istanbul. I looked at flights, read travel books, and shared my wish with friends. At the time, I wasn't in a financial situation where taking such a journey would have been probable. But amazingly, a year later I found myself in Istanbul,

staying at a lovely boutique hotel steps from the m
view of the harbor and the Hagia Sophia. My actions
to my transceiver that this was my desire and I was reau,

You'll remember that Money said, "...*most humans are not conscious that they create their lives in each moment by what they are sending and* **what they are able to receive.**" In all of my work with Money, I've realized that having open receiving channels is of the utmost importance. Most people have barriers in this channel. If there's a barrier to receiving we are consistently emotionally undernourished due to our inability to recognize the good when it comes or to take it in. So there is never a sense of satisfaction or "enough." If we create our lives moment by moment, then receiving the nourishment of those moments suffused by joy and delight is key.

The last stage of the creative cycle is completion. Receiving and completion are intimate dance partners because completion is a form of nourishment. With completion comes fulfillment and a sense of satisfaction. If one has a barrier to completion then nothing is ever finished. Those concepts, projects and ideas that never get completed still energetically pull at us, calling for our attention. As a painter, when I sign a painting, I am declaring it done and I can move on. In the creation story of Genesis, when God was finished with his creation, he declared, "It is good. It is done." Without completion, nothing is ever enough. There is never true contentment.

Understanding where you are aligned and where you are blocked in the creative cycle is key to becoming the predominant creative force in your life and effectively dancing with Money. As Money says, "*This is the key to true power.*"

Since we don't live in a vacuum, we need to recognize that there are lots of others' energies hanging out in the collective field. Like it or not, they have an impact on us. For example, when many people are aligned with fear, it's easy to misread it as your own, especially if you don't have enough awareness of your own signals. As a result, consistently maintaining an alignment with the wavelength you choose to be sending isn't always so easy. Clarity and awareness of your own transceiver will mitigate the impact of the collective energies around you. Surrounding yourself with people who hold a predominantly optimistic view of the world is a gift you give yourself.

We are all transceivers. By consciously choosing the signals you are sending and receiving and aligning with the wavelength that will bring you the most joy, you will know true power. A world of empowered, joyful people, aligning with Money as an agent for good, will significantly change our planet. Who knows—the frequency of our collective wavelength could be so high that it could even inspire world peace!

In the remainder of this section, we will explore expanding your receiving channels, connecting with divine desire, gratitude and blessings, and various dimensions of wealth. This will support you to become truly empowered as the divine creator being that you are, with a transceiver that is consistently sending signals aligned with your highest and best.

Dance Steps

Take some time to ponder your own transceiver. Think back on your life. How conscious have you been of the signals you were sending and receiving? Notice the patterns. What frequency are you consistently broadcasting into the field? Is it in alignment with what you really want? Is there a barrier to desire? Action? Nourishment and receiving? Or completion?

Journal with Money for further guidance regarding your transceiver and any barriers in the creative cycle that you might have. Consider what you are consistently sending into the field and your ability to receive.

CHAPTER 11

Opening to Receive

"Life is a banquet and most poor suckers are starving to death."

Auntie Mame

"Genius is the ability to receive from the universe."

I Ching

The Gifts of the Divine

A few years ago, during a guided imagery music session, I had a vision in which I was standing on a high hill looking down on a small village with narrow streets, brightly colored houses and, in the distance, the deep blue of the Mediterranean Sea. Beside me was a large Being dressed in beautiful flowing robes. He swept his arm across the scene saying,

> *"Look at the garden of earthly delights. Look! These are the gifts of the Divine for the humans, for all of creation. The beauty of the colors, of green grass and flowers, the air, water, sun, and the ingenuity of humans to build roads and homes. All of these gifts are from the Divine. Why can't they take it in? It's simple. There is no need to hold, to grab for stuff. No need for greed or taking. These gifts are to share. Share and the gifts multiply. "*

Pointing again to the village he continued, *"Oh, if only they all knew how loved they are, there would be no need for greed or trauma. They would know the joy of delight, the light that radiates joy. They would know the gifts of the Divine. They would fully embrace the garden of earthly delights, the tastes, smells, sights, touch, sounds. These are the gifts of the human experience. Receive. Be open to receive."*

Living Deliciously

This vision on the hill reminded me of a message I'd received in a meditation while living in China. During a difficult cultural adjustment, I sat down one morning and prayed. It wasn't a particularly reverent prayer. It was more like, "What the hell am I doing here?" The response was a booming voice saying, *"You are here to learn to live deliciously."*

Since one of my mother's favorite sayings was, "Life is a vale of tears," living deliciously or fully embracing the garden of earthly delights were foreign concepts in my childhood. But, from the Being on the hill, the booming voice in my meditation, and my work with Money, I have come to appreciate that being in a body is a profound gift. Our bodily senses are our access to being able to live deliciously. This garden of earthly delights is to be celebrated, not shunned or thought of as evil.

During my dear friend Maggie's near-death experience, she encountered a deep, profound sense of peace, but had no access to any of the sensations of being in a body. She shared, "If people only knew how precious it is to be in a body, they would relish each moment of its experience. The tastes, the smells, the beauty of a sunset, the wind against your skin, all of these sensations are moments of true delight."

As mentioned in the previous chapter, open receiving channels are key to being the predominant creative force in our lives. Yet, that's where most people are constricted. Noticing and celebrating the good already present and available in our lives expands our capacity to receive. True prosperity is not limited to how much money is in the bank. It welcomes and acknowledges the incredible banquet of earthly delights that being in a body affords us--in other words, "live deliciously."

Our ability to receive is one of the most essential elements to creating an abundant and joyously prosperous life!

My Own Muddy Receiving Channels

In my early communication with Money I was consistently admonished to open my muddy receiving channels. I had no idea how muddy they were until one Sunday afternoon. On the train coming back from a gathering, I pondered how I could satiate my hunger and get to my next commitment on time. As I walked out of the station, I saw a small group of people standing near tables laden with food. There was a huge pot of soup, bread, and fruit. The people were offering food to passersby. Some people stopped and others looked suspiciously and hurried on. A young woman behind the food table caught my eye. "Would you like some soup?"

I hesitated for a moment, and then said, "Yes." She handed me a bowl of thick, hearty soup and a piece of bread. She explained to me that this was the local chapter of an international organization called Food not Bombs, which is dedicated to food justice. Every Sunday they give away food at the entrance of the station to anyone who will accept it. Many do and others don't.

It was a cold day. The soup was delicious. Holding the bowl, I was grateful for its warmth in my hands and my belly. When I was finished, I handed her the empty bowl with a hearty thank you. When she asked if I would like more I said, "Thank you, I've had enough," and turned to leave. As I was walking away, I realized that I was still hungry!

In that moment, I understood what Money was talking about. The second oldest of eleven children, I learned early on to share. As a child, my concern around taking too much was reasonable because there wasn't much to go around. Sadly, even though I was no longer a child, my perception of my share was still really small. I saw how what I perceived was my share continued to permeate my life. It affected what I asked for and what I expected. I saw how I worried if I took too much, and while I truly believed life was a banquet, many parts of me were asking for not much more than crumbs.

The "soup incident" was profound. The experience opened my eyes to a reality I had unconsciously accepted as true that was no longer valid or real. My muddy receiving channels limited what I perceived possible and what I asked for from life. And as a result, this barrier constricted what I was able to receive.

Discovering Your Receiving "Set Point"

A common block to receiving is a limit or "set point" of how much goodness, happiness, joy, money, etc. we can allow in. If it gets too good, something "magically" happens to bring us back down to our comfort zone.

"Don't be too happy or the other shoe will drop." How many of us have heard this admonition? I'm continually amazed at how much anxiety gets activated when life gets really good. Most people are more afraid of expansion than constriction, precisely because of the collective fear of the "other shoe" dropping.

My friend Tom, a kind man with a big smile, had gone through a long period of financial struggle. He shared a profound and frightening experience of the activation of his "happiness set point." While hiking up a ridge to an overlook with mountains, flower-covered meadows and a valley in the distance, he pondered how good his life had become. His family was happy. His health was excellent. For the first time in a long time he had prosperous financial flow and fulfilling work.

He shared with me, "I had an almost compelling urge to jump off the ledge. As I looked out at the beauty before me, I thought, 'It can't get any better than this, so maybe I should kill myself now before it goes away.' I was terrified and, at the same time, I realized how limited my thinking had been. No wonder I was struggling!" Fortunately, the thought passed. With shaking knees, he turned and hiked back down the mountain. Tom had no perception of how ingrained in his psyche his happiness set point was until that fateful day.

So, how to determine your own set point? It's hard to address something that can feel so elusive. Start by noticing your internal dialogue. Do you find yourself saying things like, *"No matter what I do, I never seem to get ahead?"* Or, *"It seems that just when things are going well, something always comes along and I'm back to where I started."* Or, *"I'll always have just enough, no more."* Or, *"This is as good as it gets."*

Deep within our receiving limitations is the fundamental question "How much do I deserve?" It's not the advertising messages of "you deserve" designed to get you to buy something as a way to prove that you do deserve. Instead it asks, "Do I truly have a right to be happy? Am I enough as I am?"

One day, I received a text from Karen, a former client. "I've just made my first six figures in my business. There is so much fear coming up, I can hardly breathe. Can we talk?" I knew Karen had hit her income set point. Her receiving channels were set for six figures, no more. Unclogging her receiving channels, actively communicating with her Money guide, and revisiting some old deserving issues cleared the way for her to experience financial expansion with joy and delight.

Just like Tom, Karen had pushed up against her unconscious ceiling which, for most people, is really scary. Our paradigms have structure and boundaries. They're designed to keep us safe. It's important to realize they're not static and can change as we change. Barriers to receiving are a common phenomenon in the human experience.

A client of mine was trying to figure out how to help her mother, who suffered from extreme anxiety. She couldn't understand why her mother couldn't enjoy her life when, after many years of struggle, she now had everything she wanted and needed. My only guess was that worry was a way for her mother to control how much happiness she would allow herself to experience for fear it could be taken away.

The truth is, that just like the tides, there are ebbs and flows in life. But, a receiving set point attempts to limit the flow for fear that too much flow will only hasten the ebbs. Having open receiving channels will serve to minimize the frequency and impact of the ebbs. And, more importantly, create more peace of mind.

Withholding as a Sign of Muddy Receiving Channels

One way my muddy receiving channels manifested was through withholding. For example, creativity is something that feeds my soul. This is where my passion, joy, aliveness, and true connection to myself resides. Yet, I often struggled to give my creativity the expression my heart was aching for. There was always something more important, more urgent or pressing. I experienced it as a sort of internal wall that I couldn't get beyond. Since my passion was locked away, money's ability to dance with me in ways that made my heart sing were limited. I wasn't happy and neither was Money.

Take a moment, check in, and consider the ways you may be withholding from yourself. Do you feel guilty taking time to nourish yourself and feed your soul? Have you been longing to get a massage, but don't take the time? Or spend time in nature? Connect with a friend? Take a class? Buy fresh flowers? Paint? Play an instrument? Dance? Reconnect to a dream? What have you been aching to do, but don't let yourself do? What do you feel like you need permission to do, but don't give yourself permission for? Do you spend more time proving your worth by being "productive" than you spend enjoying your life?

Withholding only serves to give ourselves the message that we can't have what we want — that other things, or other people, are more important than we are. Muddy receiving channels affect what we ask for and expect. They keeps us locked in crumbs and lack instead of fully embracing life's banquet.

If you're an entrepreneur, it's easy to get stuck in the mindset of "I need to focus on making money before I can enjoy life." This will only serve to keep you really stuck in an unhappy grind blocking your creativity, opportunities, ideas and financial expansion. Your money will be unhappy money. And, over time, you will begin to resent your business. As your resentment towards your business grows, and there will be more struggle, which will lead to more constriction. And the cycle continues.

Barriers to nourishment

Our ability to fully receive is equal to our ability to allow ourselves to be nourished in a deep, core, fundamental way. Being in a state of "never enough" is a barrier to nourishment. If we never ask ourselves, "In this moment, what is good?" If no matter what you have, all you see is what you don't have, it is impossible to feel satisfied.

The little ways we withhold or don't/can't allow ourselves to linger in moments of joy or satisfaction are the subtle ways we say "no" to ourselves. Over-scheduling, not having boundaries around work, or procrastinating so there's no time for fun are all examples of ways that I have withheld from myself.

Our actions and decisions, moment to moment, are the messages we send to ourselves and the world around us about who we are and what we deserve, in other words, our transceiver. These are indicators of our ability to allow nourishment.

One of my mentors once said, "Every action in a relationship creates a rule, reinforces a rule, or changes a rule." This includes our actions with ourselves. It tells our parts what we can have and what to expect.

Becoming a Receptive Channel

> *"Being a receptive channel is essential to creating anything. This is not about loving money, but being receptive to good, to opportunities, to ideas, to having a lifestyle that is in alignment with your greatest good."*
>
> Money

This quote further emphasizes the importance of being a receptive channel. Our capacity to receive is the key to true happiness and wealth. When our receiving channels are blocked or have filters, it's like rain falling on parched ground, puddling on the surface, unable to be absorbed. The true essence of wealth is to have a lifestyle that's in alignment with our greatest good. Not bigger, better, or more, but one that feeds and nourishes our ability to truly flourish. If you can't recognize it when it comes, you'll be in a constant state of searching but never finding. A joyously wealthy life requires our ability to notice the good we already have , to keep what delights, and to welcome more into our lives.

Simple Ways to Expand and Clear Your Receiving Channels

Thus, the secret sauce to easily keeping your transceiver on the joy and delight wavelength is actively focusing on good, looking for and acknowledging joy in the little ways it shows up throughout the day. Staying aware will keep you on the frequency in which money loves to dance.

The following are some simple ways you can begin to expand and clear your receiving channels. By doing so, you are opening to true wealth. Money loves to flow into a receptive channel.

Joy Spotting

If you believe in angels, I highly recommend getting to know the Angel of Joy. I work with many different guides, depending on what support I need, and the Angel of Joy is my go-to throughout the day. She's amazing at helping me shift my transceiver to joy when I'm stuck in negativity. As humans, our emotions are a bit like Chicago weather: they can change in a heartbeat. Chicagoans have a saying, "If you don't like the weather, wait five minutes." If your emotions are feeling sucky, call on the Angel of Joy and ask her to infuse your field with joy.

It's helpful to know what brings you joy and bring it into your life as much as you can. *Joyful*, by Ingrid Fetell Lee, is a great resource filled with ideas for bringing more joy into your life. The book identifies numerous ways that people experience joy in various cultures, including whimsey, curves, color, beauty, order, confetti, rainbows, flowers, things that are round, and play. Lee believes that we can find moments of joy that feed our soul and bring delight throughout the day if we would just look for them. She recommends what she calls "joy spotting," which is actively bringing joy into daily life. The book includes a joy tool kit that invites the reader to identify key joyful elements in places, with people, things, and activities.

The Divine Art of Lingering

"17 seconds of pure thought is the ignition point for manifesting. If you hold a thought for 17 seconds, you set in motion that manifestation."

Abraham Hicks

Lingering in moments of goodness expands the potential of keeping your transceiver in that wavelength with greater frequency and ease.

Our senses are a chief way to access life's banquet, aka "living deliciously." From the taste of amazing food, to the beauty of a flower, to the sweet sounds of children laughing, or feeling the touch of rich luscious fabrics against our skin—all of these are invitations to linger in moments of joy, aliveness or awe. I love lingering over a wonderful cup of coffee in the morning.

When I shared the divine art of lingering with one of my clients she said, "Oh, I totally get it. If I take the time to hang out in the park and watch the birds, instead of pushing myself when I'm tired, I come back to my day in a way better mood. I have more ideas and can see more possibilities to grow my business than if I just continued to slog along. And, I'm happier."

Just as joy spotting creates the opportunity for more joy, lingering for 17 seconds on moments that are pleasing trains your brain for more positivity.

The divine art of lingering is a discipline that takes practice. It's not easy for those of us who live in a world where our busyness determines our value and worth. Learning to linger will dramatically increase your ability to create a joyously wealthy life.

I live a few blocks from a magical and stunningly beautiful rose garden with a hundred-year-old fountain of colorful ceramic geese spewing forth streams of water that glisten in the sunlight. At times, it still takes a conscious effort to remind myself to stop, bask in the beauty, and to literally "smell the roses."

Developing a Generous Spirit

Breaking down our nourishment and receiving barriers requires a shift in our relationship with ourselves. Treating ourselves with kindness and dignity is a practice that is not so often encouraged. Our critical voices are stuck in the job of reminding us of all the ways we're not enough, in an effort to make us be "enough." Bringing compassion and kindness to all the parts of ourselves is an act of generosity that will help to heal even the parts you would love to hate, inviting our true essence to be more in charge of life. Remember, every action makes a rule, reinforces a rule or changes the rule. Slowly changing the rules you live by from constriction and withholding to generosity and expansiveness creates space for more good to inhabit your life.

A generous spirit graciously receives a compliment instead of pushing it away. Open receiving channels graciously receive when others give, understanding that in the giving is receiving and in the receiving is giving. As a self-professed person with very parched receiving channels, I couldn't see, receive or take in the support that was available. It reflected a deep belief that I was all alone and there was no one to help me.

We cannot dance with Money or co-create with the Divine when we're not able to accept the support and help when it comes. The Divine works through others, but, if we push away help when it comes, life is indeed difficult and a struggle. I had no idea that my world was abundant with assistance and support until I opened my receiving channels to let it in.

Taking on a client who is not good a fit out of fear is not generous. It is often triggered by a lack of trust and blocked receiving channels. As one of my friends said recently, "The $2,500 I got from that client who was such a hassle, was so not worth it and so not an act of generosity to myself or to her." Honestly, firing a client can be one of the most powerful things one can do. It's a potent demonstration of worth, value, trust and clear receiving channels.

Shifting from withholding to being generous opens our heart, not only in our relationship with ourselves, but with others as well. Because we're not operating from lack, there is more joy, delight, abundance, and willingness. This enhances the ability to notice opportunities when they arise and take action to bring them to fruition.

Minimize Times of Struggle by Dancing with Joy and Delight

Friends of mine own a stone company that sources beautiful stones from around the world. During the real estate and economic crisis, they struggled to stay afloat. Many of their competitors were going out of business.

Instead of being in a place of despair and panic, they made a conscious decision that they would not allow the stress to destroy them. They actively searched for anything free that would keep their spirits high and helped them feel abundant and prosperous. Music, art and culture are soul-feeding activities for them. Using public transportation, they went to every free outdoor concert they could find. At the end of a night of wonderful, enlivening music, the lack and fear that surrounded their industry was no longer in their consciousness.

Business is back and booming, and so are their receiving channels. They continue to engage in the activities that fed their soul in the bad times, keeping their joy alive in the good. While struggle is definitely part of the human experience, my friends are a good example of being able to dance with joy at the same time.

A truly wealthy, rich and prosperous life starts with opening your channels to receiving. It's essential! Money needs rich soil filled with your nutrients of "enough" and deserving to have a place to grow. Since Money aches to be an agent for good, it also aches to support you to feed your soul, to generously give to yourself and others, to fully participate in the banquet of life by lingering in the good, by graciously receiving and feeding the quantum field with your gratitude and appreciation.

Remember, we create our lives in each moment, sending messages to the field. Do you welcome and invite the good, or do you push it away? Clear receiving channels say, "Bring it on!"

Dance Steps

Dialogue with Money as to ways your receiving channels are clogged. How available are you to receive? How do you withhold from yourself? Start taking little actions to honor your deeper needs and wants and that make your heart sing. Linger in moments of joy and delight. Practice kindness and respect for all the parts of you, bringing more generosity of spirit.

At the end of the day, take time to acknowledge your receiving efforts and all the good of the day. Our parts love to be praised. It's a way to gift yourself.

CHAPTER 12

Gratitude and Blessings

"....gratitude helps to enhance the flow of good into your life. It puts the emphasis on what works because what you focus on creates an attractor field for more."

Money

This chapter is actually an extension of opening to receive. A gratitude and blessings practice is so impactful that it required its own chapter.

Gathering the Good

It dawned on me the other day that *everything* in my home was there as a result of an exchange of money. From the nails and boards that held its structure in place, to the hand-made multi-colored rug from Istanbul under my feet. It was as if the buzz of all the people and money that exchanged hands still lingered in the space, even though the building is more than a hundred years old. I had an even deeper understanding that the current of money, like electricity, is alive and constantly moving.

I'd just finished reading Ken Honda's book, *Happy Money*. He postulates that the reason cities are more vibrant than the countryside is because of the continuous flow of financial exchange that's happening 24/7. In his book he defines "happy money" as that which is flowing with gratitude and blessings to and from you. Unhappy money is that which is filled with fear and anxiety, greed or lack. I wondered if all the money that flowed, in order to create my home and all the things gracing it, was happy money. If not, could I transform it by filling it with gratitude and blessings? If Money is the expression of divine love in the marketplace, I wanted its love to fill my home.

"Mentally gather all the good in your life. Find your sources of joy and delight. As you actively notice, appreciate and acknowledge them, you will bring more and more of it into your life."

Money

This lesson from Money, along with my "ah ha" regarding money's pervasive presence in my home, led to a morning practice of gathering the sources of joy and delight that lived there. I decided to choose just one thing each day and really appreciate its presence. I began with the hand-woven rug from Istanbul that I love. Opening my heart, I felt deep appreciation and joy for its beautiful colors and patterns. I felt gratitude for those who spent months weaving it, and the fact that it traveled so many miles to grace my home. My prayer of gratitude and blessings was:

"Thank you Money as the expression of Divine Source for this beauty and abundance. I bless you. As I bless you, I bless myself, I bless all that I have, and I invite those blessings to extend into the quantum field for all. Money, I invite you to dance with me this day."

"As the expression of Divine Source…" These words took me to another level of understanding around my relationship with Money. It was as if I could feel a pipeline of sparkling golden light, always present, just waiting to be called on, invited and activated. But, I had to be willing to tap in, turn on the faucet, and allow it to flow.

Gratitude

In the last chapter, I shared the concept of the Divine Art of Lingering. While lingering is about savoring the moment, adding gratitude to your lingering gives it a power punch. According to the Heartmath Institute[9], a non-profit that scientifically studies the power of the heart, gratitude and appreciation immediately puts the heart into coherence. Being in a state of gratitude is a powerful antidote to fear and anxiety. It opens the heart and calms the mind, creating more access to heart wisdom and intuition.

As I write this, I am noticing the comfortable chair I'm sitting in, the Earl Grey tea, warm and delicious on the table next to me, the buzz of conversation in the sweet patisserie that surrounds me. All of these seemingly small things help to create an environment that feeds my spirit and my creative self.

The power of gratitude is that it creates a virtual container that holds the vibration of what you personally find pleasing. Sitting in a patisserie and having a cup of tea in the afternoon may not be something that would delight you. But, since I am gratefully noticing it, I'm creating my own vessel of pleasure and delight.

Having a consistent gratitude practice has many benefits. According to UC Davis gratitude researcher, Robert Emmons, PhD: "Gratitude enriches human life. It elevates, energizes, inspires and transforms. People are moved, opened and humbled through expressions of gratitude."[10] Emmons also found that gratitude actually raises one's happiness set point, which we explored in the last chapter.

A few years ago, I'd invested in a few programs for my business that were not delivering what I'd hoped. When I tried to get a refund, there

---

9   www.heartmath.org

10   *Thanks: How the New Science of Gratitude Can Make You Happier,* by Robert Emmons

was no response. The issue was keeping me up at night as I ruminated in shame, anger, and anxiety.

Lying in bed one morning, berating myself yet again, I suddenly stopped. Thankfully, I was able to disengage enough to recognize that all the angst I was creating was not helping the situation. It only served to make me more miserable. I decided to follow my own guidance, shift my focus, and thank Money for the good already in my life. I was in a hotel room with a really comfortable bed. I thanked Money for the comfort. It was incredibly cold outside, but toasty inside. I thanked Money for the heat. As I took time to notice the little things that I was grateful for, my heart opened. I felt wealthy and blessed. My anxiety "magically" disappeared and I knew everything would be okay. I didn't get my money back. Pondering why I'd bought the programs in the first place, I realized the purchase was made in a moment of lack. I took the gift of the lesson and gratefully moved on.

Our brains naturally create neural pathways with similar thoughts and resulting actions. Gratitude will enable your transceiver to maintain more joy and delight, enhance your receiving channels and connect you with desire. It also begins to train your brain to notice what is working, creating new neural pathways that support more positivity. By identifying your sources of joy and delight, actively noticing and acknowledging them, you'll bring more of that to your life. Remember, energy flows to where attention goes.

In research psychologist Richard Wiseman's book *The Luck Factor*, he writes that lucky people tend to focus on what works. They consistently find the gift in any situation and consider themselves lucky because, no matter how difficult the circumstances they experienced, they know it could have been worse. Because these people look for the good, the good tends to come to them. Those who look for luck and synchronicities see the world as connected and find that the world responds in kind.

Blessings

"A blessing draws potentiality into actuality..... Blessings are powerful. When one person blesses another, it's as if the person blessing reads the other's soul purpose and prays for it to be realized."

Rabbi Douglas Goldhamer

Gratitude, combined with blessings, raises your vibration, activates potential and creates a powerful attractor field for expansive, joyous delight. The result is a prosperous flow that invites Money to join with you. Setting your transceiver to the gratitude and blessings dial creates a wavelength that attracts more of what you really want, because you're telling the field, "This is what delights my soul, thank you!" Gratitude is one of the most powerful ways to reconnect to your essential self.

But, what are blessings and why are they so are they so powerful? For myself, growing up Catholic, blessings were integral to many prayers. The prayer before meals asked for blessings for the gift of food and for ourselves. Animals and homes had special blessing prayers. Additionally, in the Jewish tradition, numerous prayers call on blessings and the priestly blessing from a Rabbi is one of the most powerful blessings one can receive.

I'd heard the word *"blessings"* from Money long before I came across the above quote from Kabbalistic Rabbi Douglas Goldhamer. Even though I wasn't sure why, it seemed like a good idea. So I started sending blessings to everyone and everything, including Money.

"A blessing draws potentiality into actuality..." When I read these words in Goldhamer's book, *Healing with God's Love,* I understood the importance and power of blessings. Blessings are an activator! If I send blessings to money, I am activating its pure potential as an agent for good and the expression of Divine Love in the market place. If I send blessings to my day, I am activating the pure potential of the day.

If gratitude creates attractor fields for more of what you're grateful for, then blessings are what activates it. It's the ignitor! It's a powerful combination. Gratitude and blessings!

Infusing your days with blessings, inviting Money to dance with you and blessing all the ways money flows to and from you enhances its connection to divine source. This phenomenon is intimately connected to making sure your transceiver is open and ready to send and receive all the goodness of life.

Having gratitude for all the blessings that money provides invites more of the same. Additionally, blessing your money invites it to fulfill its pure potential, as an agent for good, *everywhere* your money travels. Blessing yourself invites the activation of your potential. Blessing those you love invites the same for them. Blessing your life invites your highest and best to come to you with ease and grace.

Blessing our money not only invites its potential in our life, it also invites our potential as far as our relationship with it. It elevates money to something that can support and care for us and those we love, and as something worthy of being blessed.

Blessing money can actually bring out its holiness. We invite it to be an agent for generous and collaborative systems in the world that nourish our individual and collective souls and sustain the planet.

Dance Steps

Adding gratitude and blessings to your receiving practice will greatly expand your receiving capabilities and keep your transceiver's ability to receive higher frequencies. Dialogue with your Money guide to get more clarity on the power of gratitude and blessings for yourself.

Consider starting your day with the morning practice shared at the beginning of this chapter. You can send blessings to the day, to all of your interactions, particularly your money interactions, and the day's intentions.

As mentioned in the last chapter, linger in moments of joy throughout the day. Activate them with appreciation and blessings. Continue to engage in activities that make your heart sing, and practice generously giving and receiving.

At the end of the day, take time to notice the good, the synchronicities, the "lucky" things that happened, what you appreciated or felt gratitude for. Include times when you felt rich from life and its gifts. Include the smallest things. Put those things in your appreciation container.

CHAPTER 13

Desire is Divine

"Trust in dreams, for in them is the hidden gate to the sublime."

Khalil Gibran

"Cherish your visions and your dreams as they are the children of your soul, the blueprints of your ultimate achievements."

Napoleon Hill

Divine Desire

Our *true desires*, bubbling up from the heart, form the guide to our true expression in the world. They guide us to walk the path we came to walk. It's the desire ascending deep from the core of our being that stirs us to take the action needed to fulfill our destiny.

Desire is the divine motivator inspiring our unique expression in its many forms. Without the desire to express there would be no art, music, design, beauty, amazing food, books, children, or the advancement of ideas brought into reality. It was the desire of the Creator to express Itself that brought us and all of creation into existence. Being able to usher into reality that which is aligned with our joy is truly holy. It is the expression of our own divinity.

Connecting with what we truly desire, arising from the urgings of our soul, is essential in creating a joyous life. When our receiving channels are open and desire is conscious we are not locked in limitation. We have *a full palette of possibility from which to choose.*

Unfortunately, desire has gotten a bad rap. Like money, it's been accused of being one of the biggest sources of pain and anguish in life. Many religious traditions preach about the need to rise above desires and totally detach from wanting. But, it is not desire that brings the pain and angst desire has been blamed for, it's attachment to the outcome. For example, if being truly wealthy is only represented by a black two-door sport Mercedes, then nothing but the Mercedes will fill the hole. But, is it really the Mercedes or the need to feel powerful, admired, and successful that the Mercedes is supposed to provide? Without having clarity about the true why behind a desire, attachment to the outcome is inevitable.

Barriers to Desire

Years ago, I was walking through Costco with a friend and her two-year old son. We came across a display of toy trucks. There were bright green dump trucks, fiery red fire trucks and sleek silver semi-trucks. My friend's son was fascinated. He begged his mom for a truck. When she asked him which one he wanted, without hesitation he said, "The dump truck."

I was stunned at the fact that this kid knew exactly what he wanted, since I often had no clue. It dawned on me that at two, I must have known also. Pretty much every two-year-old I know has a very clear idea what they want or don't want.

Curious, I asked myself, "What happened?" I realized that as a child growing up in a large family, there often wasn't enough to go around. As a result, some part of me decided that what I wanted didn't matter because I wasn't going to get it anyway. It wasn't that I didn't deserve it. It just wasn't going to happen.

Recently, at a networking event, someone said, "I think most people have no clue what they want." I piped up, "I don't agree. They may not consciously know what they want, but deep down inside everyone knows what they want. It's just that when you believe you can't have it, you block yourself from knowing. It's much less painful to not know what you want, than to know what you want and think you can't have it."

That's what happened to me. I'd created a part of me whose job was to disconnect me from my heart's true desire. My heart was still chatting, but I couldn't hear it. When we don't listen, the volume gets turned down. It's like a radio that's still broadcasting but the signal isn't coming through.

The Price of Disconnection

Being disconnected from true desire creates vulnerability to outside influences telling us what we should want, be, or have. When I taught consumer behavior, one of the students' test questions was, *"Do marketers create needs or wants?"* The answer was *wants*. Too often wants are created by the subtle but pervasive marketing messages that these things will make you happy, belong, be "enough", loved... in other words, "fit in."

It is not our soul's desire that those messages are speaking to, but to the parts of us that ache to be "enough", to be seen, to be celebrated, and to know that the world is a safe place. Because they're speaking to the deepest needs of human existence, we become confused as to what is truly our soul's desire and what we think we *should* want. **What we think we should want, instead of what we really want, become the coats we wear without bothering to ask if they are the right color, style or fit for us.**

Unfortunately, we're increasingly inundated by marketing images telling us that if we have this thing or look a particular way, then we will be loved, powerful, successful, wealthy, safe, belong, etc. They feed a deep sense of dissatisfaction and attachment.

It's easy to fall into the downward spiral of social comparison. Looking outside ourselves for what we think we should want or should have only serves to lock us into feelings of lack, failure, and the drive to prove that we have value and worth. The resulting dissatisfaction only serves to block our receiving channels from taking in the wealth that's already in our lives and giving us access to our true desires. It is a heavy cost.

Clarity vs. "Abundance"

One day a client came to my office complaining, "I am praying for abundance every day and nothing is changing." I laughed, "Would you go to a restaurant and say, 'Just give me whatever you have and make sure it's a lot?' This is exactly what you are doing when you pray for abundance."

Contrary to popular belief, *asking for abundance is not clarity*. It's like telling the Universe, "You figure out what I want, because I'm not willing to figure it out myself." We are abdicating our will and our desires and it's often for fear of asking. It's kind of like, "If I don't really ask, I won't be disappointed." One day, a colleague and I decided to open the Akashic Field of abundance. It was a very strange experience. I sensed into a very oddly amorphous and nebulous energy. There was little form or structure. As we tried to connect with it, it seemed to shift and morph. I laughed and said, "No wonder asking for abundance brings no results." As a result, I began to understand, with even greater clarity, the importance of being definitive.

Are you sending "I want abundance" through your transceiver? You very well could get abundance of anything including stress, struggle, etc. Not so good, huh? Clarity of desire is the key to manifesting what you really want.

"You must become aware of what you are sending and receiving."

Money

Qualities vs. Exact Form

Kit had been sleeping on the couch for way too long. At the time, giving her daughters their own room felt like the best solution to the fighting provoked by sharing one. But, Kit felt trapped and poor on the couch. She didn't sleep well, and because the couch was her bed, no one felt comfortable sitting on it. The situation was affecting her self-esteem and her ability to make money because she felt stuck. Being able to afford a three-bedroom apartment felt like an impossibility, which made her feel even more stuck.

Together we explored the qualities she was looking for in a home. She said, "I want to look out on green plants and nature, bedrooms for everyone, comfortable living spaces, and convenience to my kids' school."

I asked her which of those qualities she already had in her current space. She admitted that she loved the neighborhood she was living in. It was convenient and close to a lot of what was important to her, including her children's school and their father. Visiting her home, I could see that Kit could have all the features she ached for in a home without the hassle of moving. Because she was so focused on moving, she couldn't see the potential that was already there.

We moved the furniture in creative ways to utilize the space more efficiently. I invited her to buy plants for the balcony outside her window. The dining room was transformed into her bedroom with the help of a beautiful screen. No longer mom's bed, her daughters now enjoyed hanging on the couch. The cat, who had been segregated in the former dining room, was now part of the family with his perch where people congregated. Money began to flow! Kit's apartment was transformed and so was the feeling of possibility. She got what she wanted in ways she'd never imagined. When she walked into her home now, it felt prosperous and wealthy. She loved climbing into her new bed and even began to consider dating again.

We don't have to wait to begin to bring the qualities of what we truly want into our lives. In Kit's case, by connecting to the qualities she wanted to bring into her life and being creative, she was able to create the feeling she wanted her home to impart to her and her daughters. It wasn't the beyond-budget, three-bedroom apartment in the exclusive suburb she *thought* she wanted. Kit had all of what she *really* wanted.

As mentioned earlier, attachment to how things are supposed to look is where desire gets its bad rap. Many people chase after an image instead of connecting to the deeper feeling that the desire wants to have expressed in their life. For Kit, by not having to move and take on additional financial struggle, she was able to feel a greater sense of ease. Her heart was singing and she had all the qualities she'd desired.

The "I Can't Afford It" Shutdown

Too many people use "I can't afford that," as a way to shut down desire. It's a very powerful way to immediately tell ourselves,' "Don't even bother because you're not going to get it anyway." This is not about spending or not, as there is a separate chapter on spending later in this book. It's about the power of our words and their impact on us. Something else to say that implies choice is, "It's not in the budget right now." Or, "How *can* I afford it?"

True desire needs to be able to flourish and dream and to live from choice instead of lack. In Kit's case, by getting clear on the qualities she desired, she was able to create it. Additionally, she wanted a home she could easily afford without stress and more options and she got it.

At a money retreat I asked participants, "How would your life be different if you were wealthy? What would you do, be or have?" The next question was, "What are the qualities that this would give you?" After everyone was done, we put the qualities on a huge sheet of paper. They were things like adventure, beauty, connection, fulfillment, etc. "Do you need money to begin to bring this into your life right now?" The answer was a resounding, "No!" Which is why I am saying, you don't have to wait to have a wealthy life. This not only opens your receiving channels, it gives your unconscious mind the message that life is already wealthy, which creates even more of a sense of wealth. As you feel into desire, you may find that much of what you truly desire you already have. You just didn't know it.

For example, Jillian came to me for an intuitive consult to help her with her relationship with money. She complained that her income had dropped as a result of closing one of her businesses because it wasn't bringing her joy. In the meantime, she'd been hired to be a travel writer for an upscale magazine that featured high-end spas in Asia. She shared with me that she had been staying at five-star spas, getting five-star treatments and traveling first class. All of these things she wouldn't have been able to experience with her other business because it took a lot of her time.

I looked at her and said, "Money is gifting you with these amazingly wealthy experiences that you're not paying for, someone else is." Unfortunately, because she wasn't paying for it herself, she didn't see that money was actually flowing in the form of an incredibly wealthy lifestyle. She traveled, she met interesting people, she was respected for her work and she had five-star treatment. These were all things that brought her joy. Money was definitely dancing with her!

Learning to Listen to Your Heart

At a networking event, I was talking to a young woman who complained she wasn't happy, but had no idea what she really wanted. My response was, "Can you give yourself twenty minutes a day? I will give you an exercise that will help you listen to your heart." Sadly, her answer was,

"I'm not sure, I'm so busy." It made me think of this quote from *Alice in Wonderland*, as Alice speaks with the Cheshire Cat.

> *"Would you tell me, please, which way I ought to go from here?"* *"That depends a good deal on where you want to get to." "I don't much care where." "Then it doesn't matter which way you go."*

Lewis Carroll

True desire is our true north. If your heart is not singing, you have disconnected from desire, decided you couldn't afford to be happy, or are just too busy to listen. By making the care and feeding of your heart and soul a priority, doors will begin to open. But, if you've never been taught to listen to your heart, then how to do it?

This is the exercise I shared with the young woman. If you have no clue what you really want, or have a hard time listening to your heart, this will support you to reconnect with your heart's desire and with what brings you happiness and joy. It will require twenty minutes of your day. Ten minutes in the morning and ten at night. You will also need a journal to write in.

In the morning:

Set a timer for ten minutes. Sit in a comfortable chair. Close your eyes and take a few slow breaths. Put your hand on your heart and think of something or someone you appreciate. Allow that sense of appreciation to fill your chest. Now ask your heart. "Heart, what do you want? What do you really desire?" Just listen. Write down anything you hear. Close your eyes and ask the same question. Do this until the ten minutes are done.

At the end of the day:

Think back on the day and ask yourself, in what way was my life wealthy? What brought me joy and what made my heart sing? Document your findings in your journal.

Do these exercises at least two weeks before reading your journal. You will begin to see patterns and feel a deep sense of reconnection to what really matters to you.

The clearer you are, the quicker what you truly desire will show up.

In my work with money I have come not just to believe, but to know, that love, joy, and delight are our birthright and that of all creation. But until we can identify what will delight, what will inspire passion, bring fulfillment, and all the other experiences that will nourish our souls, it's easy to be buffeted by what we *think* we want. We cannot create anything with consistency. We cannot ask clearly for what we need and allow it into our lives.

Dance Steps

In reconnecting to desire, ask yourself, "If my life was wealthy, what would it look like? Where would I live? What would I be doing differently? What would I have?" Really ponder these questions and set aside time to dream. Would you travel more? Would you move? How would you spend your free time?

For each of your answers, identify the deep desire and qualities that they would bring into your life. It could be adventure, beauty, comfort, connection, ease, passion, fun, serenity—any number of things. If beauty is one of them, feel into the feeling of beauty. How do you experience that in your body? What is it about beauty that feels wealthy to you? Can you begin to bring beauty into your life right now?

> *Begin to bring more of the feeling states of wealth into your life. Remember to focus on what you really want, not on the money you think is required to buy it. There are many ways for situations to manifest without having to pay for them.*

Give thanks for what is already present in your life. In addition, give thanks in advance for the good that is on its way.

Feeling into desire in its divine state will guide you in amazing and astonishing ways. Ultimately it's creating your wealthy life on your own terms. That's true freedom. In the next chapter we'll explore all the various dimensions of wealth beyond money that are necessary for a wealthy, prosperous, joyous life.

CHAPTER 14

Dimensions of Joyous Wealth

"Wealth is the ability to fully experience life."

Henry David Thoreau

If inviting a nourishing and joyously wealthy life as we dance with money is what we are ultimately creating, then the question becomes what is joyous wealth? Curious about the origins of the word *wealth*, I was amazed and delighted to discover it is derived from the old English word "weal," meaning well-being.[11] Exploring the idea further, I found a powerful definition of well-being on the Australian government's website on health, "Well-being is … a complex combination of a person's physical, mental, emotional and social factors. Well-being is strongly linked to happiness and life satisfaction."[12]

If well-being and wealth are intimately connected, then wealth is not just about money, but a lifestyle filled with meaning, connection, joy, and the ability to fulfill one's potential. Too many people live with the false belief they have to wait until they have lots of money in the bank in order to be happy and actually enjoy life. *The truth is, once one's basic needs are met, more money does not equal more happiness.*

I hear too many people bemoan their supposed lack, with "If only I had enough money, I would …." As we explored in the desire chapter, you don't have to wait. You can start now, because the qualities needed for well-being are not dependent on large quantities of money and, at the same time,

---

11 https://en.wiktionary.org/wiki/wealth

12 https://www.betterhealth.vic.gov.au/health/healthyliving/wellbeing

money provides the support to realize them. Committing to your well-being means understanding and attending to all the areas of life needed for well-being. Together they create a lovely whole that's greater than the sum of its parts. When everything is in place, the result is a joyously wealthy life that delights the soul, creates happiness and honors our divine desire

Dimensions of Joyous Wealth & Well-Being

Spiritual Wealth

> *"Life is not primarily a quest for pleasure, as Freud believed, or a quest for power, as Alfred Adler taught, but a quest for meaning. The greatest task for any person is to find meaning in his or her life."*

Victor Fankl

Spiritual wealth is our connection to passion, purpose, and meaning. It aligns our soul's intention to be in human form with its expression in the world. It connects our gifts to the marketplace. It guides our decisions to be good stewards of the planet, of money and of all creation. It brings a greater sense of mission and becomes the GPS of our lives. With strong spiritual wealth, the result is clarity, confidence, and the ability to navigate the waters of life, no matter how rough they may be.

In *Before Happiness*, happiness researcher Shawn Achor writes about the importance of finding meaning as a precursor to happiness. According to Achor, the more places of meaning we have in our lives, the more it expands our happiness channels.

Without a clear sense of purpose, life becomes filled with empty activities in an attempt to fill the hole that disconnection from our soul creates. There are many instances of people driven to create huge financial empires, only to find their life devoid of meaning in the end. More possessions won't bring more happiness, peace of mind, or love.

If you are reading this book, you more than likely have spiritual wealth. And, since money and spirituality are not often dancing together, a common belief is that money is not spiritual. Truly, money, as many of us have known it, stuck in the old paradigm of domination and greed, was not reflective of spiritual values. *Yet, it is important to realize that money is one of our greatest spiritual teachers. It clearly shows us our beliefs, limitations, fears, and our areas of growth.*

By truly understanding spiritual wealth, money can now be welcomed as an agent for good. There is no need to choose between money and a strong spiritual connection. Being human is fully embraced as something the soul chose to experience for its growth. Since money is a magnifier, money and spiritual wealth are a great combination. What an amazing world it would be if a majority of people with a high degree of financial and spiritual wealth were a dominant force for good!

Relationship and Connection Wealth

> *"We don't accomplish anything in this world alone...*
> *Whatever happens is the result of the whole tapestry*
> *of one's life and the weavings of individual threads*
> *from one to another, that creates something."*

Sandra Day O'Connor

One of the reasons solitary confinement is so detrimental to a person's health is that well-being *requires* connection. On Maslow's hierarchy of needs, once the basics of food and shelter are met, belonging is essential. With connection wealth, we have people who see and celebrate us. We feel supported and held. We know we are enough.

A strong sense of community and the ability to maintain intimate, loving relationships are key to both emotional and physical health. In his book, *Outliers*, Malcolm Gladwell writes about a small town in Pennsylvania where people had a surprising lack of common age-related issues, such as heart disease and high blood pressure. Initially, their diet was thought to be the reason. But after further investigation, it was discovered that most of the citizens came from the same small town in Italy. There were numerous community organizations in which people actively participated. Instead of the olive oil that researchers originally proposed, it was actually relationship wealth that kept these people healthy and strong, with greater longevity.

Those with strong connection wealth have greater self-esteem, greater empathy for others, and are more trusting and cooperative. This creates a well-being feedback loop because, as a result, others are more open, trusting, and cooperative in return.

Relationship wealth is a key component to success in life. In Feng Shui, (feng shway) an ancient Chinese art of placement, if you want to make more money you enhance your helpful people corner. Being an incredibly practical culture, it is understood in China that without the help and support of others, wealth and happiness are unattainable.

Additionally, in Chinese there is a special word for relationships, guan xi. (gwan shee) It refers to the social networks and influential relationships that facilitate business and open doors. Without guan xi, success is almost impossible. There are many stories of Western companies who unsuccessfully attempted to launch in Asian markets, not understanding that establishing a relationship was the essential precursor to a contract.

Relationship wealth extends to those we hire. To be focused on the bottom line at the expense of those who support us does not honor money, nor does it honor you. It is a form of relationship poverty.

When hiring people, I will always ask, Of all the services you provide, which do you love to do?" Those are the things I have them do. Money loves us to hire people to do what they love. It gifts them and it gifts us because they will bring their best self to their work. Paying generously for their time opens the flow for more to come back to us in return.

These are all examples of relationship wealth: taking time to be with family and friends; asking for and accepting support; giving your love and support; and becoming active in community organizations.

Treating everyone with whom you come in contact with dignity and respect will greatly enhance your relationship wealth. My hairdresser is as an important an asset in my life as my global connections and colleagues. By feeding and nourishing your relationships with your time and attention you feed not only your relationships but also yourself.

Connection wealth means feeling a sense of belonging and place on the planet. One way to increase this is to give, share, and offer support to others. Simple things like volunteering or belonging to a book club or community organization are easily accessible ways to increase connection wealth. In *Before Happiness,* happiness researcher Shawn Achor invites people to become positivity geniuses by sharing smiles and acts of kindness as a way to increase overall wellbeing. True connection wealth is a big key to the happiness so many are aching for.

Emotional Well-Being Wealth

"Joy, rather than happiness, is the goal of life, for joy is the emotion which accompanies our fulfilling our natures as human beings. It is based on the experience of one's identity as a being of worth and dignity."

Rollo May

It's difficult to consider whether having all the other dimensions of wealth in place creates emotional well-being, or that emotional well-being facilitates the creation of the other dimensions. The threads are intricately intertwined, particularly in connection to relationship and spiritual wealth.

When we feel emotional well-being, we feel confident, "enough", and valued. We are safe in our skin and safe in the world. We treat our self with utmost kindness and dignity. We honor our hopes and dreams and are able to take the action we need in order to make them a reality. We can make money with joy and share it freely with our community, family and selves, while also having a balance in savings.

Many of us ache to be truly seen and celebrated just for who we are because we never got it as a child. Being in the company of people who are safe to be with, who give us a sense of belonging through relationship wealth, described above, brings a precious gift to our lives and further as enhances emotional well-being.

With emotional well-being wealth, we are connected to our intrinsic value and the mastery we bring to the marketplace. Money happily reflects it back to us in the form of flow. As we live more from our essential Self, as honored in many spiritual traditions and more specifically in the Internal Family Systems model, we have greater access to its wonderful qualities. Qualities such as creativity, compassion, clarity, courage, confidence and more. I like to think that when we are operating from our essential Self, we hold an identity that is fundamentally wealthy. There is nothing to prove. No need to compare. Lack and fear do not dominate one's existence. There is a deep connection to enough. Money and a strong wealth identity are able dance together generously and prosperously.

Right Work Wealth

Hide not your Talents, they for Use were made.
What's a Sun-Dial in the shade!

Benjamin Franklin

My friend and brilliant gifts coach, Brian Jaudon, believes that our gifts choose us, we don't choose them. Expressing our divine gifts and talents in the world is one of the most satisfying ways that money loves to flow to us. Bringing your gifts to the marketplace is an act of self-love and making love to the world. Right work wealth is such an essential dimension of wealth for money's flow, it needs its own chapter, which you will find later in this book.

Health Wealth

"Do something every day that is loving towards your body..."

Golda Poretsky

Our body is the temple of our soul. Through it we experience the joys of the garden of earthly delights—for example, a sunset, phenomenal food, the scent of a rose, the sound of children laughing, the touch of a lover. All of these sensations are gifts of being human.

Acts of kindness and love towards ourselves greatly enhances both our emotional and physical health and are a form of well-being. I once heard Deepak Chopra, medical doctor and spiritual guru, say that all metabolic functioning begins with thought.

Health wealth requires loving yourself enough to care for your body. Our bodies need physical activity, nourishing food, loving attention, and sleep. Our body is the vehicle our soul uses to have a human experience and to be in a body is truly a gift. According to the Kabbalah, a form of mystical Judaism, every cell in our body has its own soul and intelligence.

If you have physical health wealth, be grateful—guard it and attend to it. Bless and thank your body for attending to you and your soul's path. Thank all your organs for the amazing job they do. Give them the vitamins, food, leisure, play, rest and the exercise they need to sustain you.

Rejuvenation Wealth

We will be more successful in all our endeavors if we can let go of the habit of running all the time, and take little pauses to relax and re-center ourselves. And, we'll also have a lot more joy in living."

Thich Nhat Hanh

Being able to nourish and rejuvenate ourselves without guilt is a form of wealth. It's not just for our body, it's also for our well-being. Rejuvenation and free time wealth give us the space to think, ponder, create, enjoy, nurture and nourish ourselves. We are able to "be" instead of just "do." When we engage in nourishing and life enhancing experiences that are beyond accumulating more things, life becomes delicious and luscious.

Unfortunately, productivity, as an indicator of value and worth, permeates many cultures. According to cultural anthropologist, Clotaire Rapaille,[13] the culture code for work in the United States, is "who I am," meaning our very identity is tied to our work. Taking the value of

13 Rapaille, Clotaire. *The Culture Code, An Ingenious Way to Understand Why People Around the World Live and Buy as They Do. 2007*

productivity to the extreme is the Japanese culture which actually has a word for death from overwork – Keroshi.

During a session, Elaine complained of exhaustion and feeling overworked. I invited her to be curious and ask herself what she was afraid would happen if she took time to rest and nourish herself. Just pondering self-care brought on a wave of guilt. She remembered being constantly praised as a child for how much she accomplished. She had also heard her father deride people who didn't work hard as lazy. As a result, she was terrified of being lazy.

"Do you think you have a part that's lazy?" I asked. Elaine hesitated, "Yes, I guess I do, but I work hard at keeping her away."

"Could it be possible that part is actually not lazy, but wants to help you have fun and enjoy life? Maybe inviting her to be more present in your life could be helpful."

The suggestion that enjoying life was not lazy was a revelation to Elaine, who'd spent her life trying to prove that she wasn't lazy at a cost to her emotional and physical health. Her so-called lazy part transformed into a guide for more joy and fun.

While food and rest are a few ways we give ourselves energy, playful activity is another. Much research regarding the healing powers of play has emerged over the last few years, including the finding that it utilizes both hemispheres of our brains. Activities that are fun and playful bring an immediate reduction in stress and cortisol levels. "It is in playing and only in playing that the individual child or adult is able to be creative and to use the whole personality, and it is only in being creative the individual discovers the self." (Winnicott, 1971).

Lately I've been stopping at a children's playlot during my walks. Just watching children play not only brings me joy, but helps remind me of the art of playful abandon that children still know. The curiosity with which they explore all the various elements in the playlot inspires me to invite more of that into my own life.

Rejuvenation wealth can come in many forms. It can be spending time in nature, dancing, singing, traveling, getting a massage, meditating, painting, listening to or playing music, participating in theater, and any other activity that truly feeds and nourishes your mind, body and spirit.

What nourishes your soul? What brings a sense of well-being and rejuvenation? What inspires joy and passion?

Environmental Wealth

> *I want my home to be that kind of place--a place*
> *of sustenance, a place of invitation, a place of welcome.*

Mary DeMuth, *Live Uncaged*

Gifting yourself with an environment that feels nurturing, beautiful and intentional doesn't require a huge home. In her wildly popular book, *The Life Changing Magic of Tidying Up*, Marie Kondo invites the reader to surround herself with only those things that bring joy. A home filled only with joy would truly be wealthy home!

Look around your home. Are there things that pull at you from another life? That don't fit? That feel shabby or make you feel constricted? This is a form of environmental poverty. We are connected to everything we own through little connecting strands. They speak to us and give us messages that affect our sense of self and self-esteem.

"I hate my couch." Karen's emotion was intense. "Every time I walk into my home, the first thing I see is this couch. It reminds me of all the mistakes I made while on this couch and of endless fights with my ex-husband."

I asked her why she couldn't get rid of it. Her answer was that the couch had been very expensive and she should be grateful to own it, in spite of the fact that it made her feel bad every time she walked into her home. I encouraged her to put an ad on Craig's list and give it to someone who would love it as much as she hated it. A young couple called within hours of posting the ad. Just starting out their life together, they were so excited to have the couch. Indeed, they loved it as much as she hated it.

For the next few months, Karen sat on folding chairs until she was able to afford the handmade blue velvet couch, which she loves, that is now in her home. She reported, "Every time I walk in the door, I smile. I love my new couch. It feels so luscious and wealthy." The old couch held her captive to old memories and an old identity that didn't fit who she was becoming.

I worked with an organizer years ago, giving her the tagline, "I create the flow so your money will grow." It was true that after she was finished creating organization and flow, people's financial situations began to change. Clutter creates stagnant energy, both financially and mentally.

Take a moment and walk around your home. Imagine that you are walking into it for the first time. Who is the person that lives here? What is this home saying about them? Does it feel comfortable? Is it cluttered? Does it feel happy and inviting or constricted and rigid?

Financial Wealth and Well-Being

Financial well-being is the freedom and ease of knowing you will be cared for and there will always be enough. Money is welcomed and experienced as a loving and generous force in your life. Those who constantly worry about money, cling to it, clutch it, are penurious and tight, do not have financial wealth, no matter how much money is in the bank. This is actually a form of poverty, a poverty of spirit. True financial wealth has no fear or angst around money. It is generous and expansive.

Unfortunately, poverty of spirit only serves to propagate the financial inequity that is becoming increasingly more dominant in many countries. It serves no one, for as we've explored in a previous chapter *no one* in countries with high financial inequity is immune to inequity's insidious effects .

For many, it is easy to get lulled into "the money is too good." For example, Adam's job was so stressful it triggered a severe illness that could have cost him his life. Assigned to work on a project for a company that was both difficult to work with and a big chemical polluter, it deeply compromised his integrity, sense of worth and then his health. He felt stuck because "The money is too good." I encouraged him to see that he had options, which began with asking to be taken off the project. His request was granted. His body, his spirit and the money flowing to him are now happy.

There are many ways for money to grow and flow. Financial wealth includes being willing to understanding the power of money and investing it wisely in companies that allow money to be an agent for good in the world.

Money loves attention. It loves to grow and give you the delicious life that feeds your soul and allows you to be generous with yourself and those you love. It loves attention, not from a place of fear and constriction, but from honoring its place in your life and the world. It wants to assist you in having all of the other forms of wealth. Money also loves generosity and a generosity of spirit. Once in a money retreat, one of participants raised her hand saying, "Before coming here, I gave a dollar to a homeless man on the street. What if he uses it for alcohol?" My response was, "Why is that your problem? He gave you the gift of opening your heart. That is enough. What he does with the money has nothing to do with you." Generosity is a gift we give ourselves as it is a soul feeding activity. Giving without attachment honors that in the giving we, too, are receiving.

As your relationship with Money as guide and friend deepens, you'll be able to experience true financial wealth and well-being. It's a spiritual relationship intimately connected to Divine Source and your willingness to be a good steward of the divinity as it is expressed through money.

Dance Steps

Take some time to ponder how your life is already wealthy. Which dimensions of wealth need more attention and which ones feel like they're already fully expressed? Dialogue with your Money guide regarding simple steps you can take to create an even more joyously wealthy life. As suggested in the last chapter, continue the practice of at the end of the day asking yourself, "How was my life wealthy today?" Bless the good.

Dancing with Money in the Marketplace – Flowing Out and In

CHAPTER 15

Conscious Mindful Spending

"Too many people spend the money they earned to buy things they don't want, to impress people that they don't like."

Will Rogers

"Conscious spending isn't restrictive; it's liberating. It can help you recognize when your spending is aligned with your values, and when it's just being made out of habit."

J.D. Roth

The Spending Trance

Okay, we've all done it. Standing in the checkout line, you end up with something you hadn't thought you wanted, but you just "have to have." On my last trip to Eddie Bauer the cool multi-colored hiking poles were calling to me. I had them in my hand, looked them over, and brought them to the checkout counter. As the woman was ringing up my other purchases, my partner looked at me and said, "Why are you buying them?" Honestly, I didn't have a good answer other than they looked cool. (I'm also an artist, so multi-colored cool will definitely activate my "have to have" parts.) Truthfully, in all the years I've hiked, there have been very few times I'd ever needed hiking poles. I don't live in a mountainous area, so most of my hiking is walking up gentle hills or on flat ground. I didn't realize I was in a trance until my partner asked me why I was buying them. Just taking a moment to pause and ask myself if I really needed the hiking poles was enough to break the trance. I put them back on the rack, finished my other purchases and walked out.

Trance spending can be the impulse purchase at the checkout counter, buying things you don't really need or want because they're on sale, buying to impress, trying to make feelings go away, or just that you "deserve" it.

How do we go into the trance? We all have our own trance triggers. Obviously, one of mine was aesthetics—the pretty, colorful qualities of the hiking poles. Another is interesting magazines at the checkout counter. There's a reason why there are so many things to look at near the check-out counter and why this placement promotes "impulse" buying. In other words, trance buying. Marketers know waiting in line is boring and most people would prefer to have something to fill the time. Both your defenses and rational thought are powered down.

For many, it's the experience of shopping that can put us into a trance. While living in China, one of my favorite places was the night market. People would magically appear just as the sun was setting with carts laden with lots of little things. They would park their carts under twinkling lights strung from poles. Everything from socks to electronics could be bought at the night market. It wasn't just the objects, but the entire *experience* of the night market that was so much fun—the people, the sounds, and all of the little elements. There typically was nothing I wanted to buy, but I would look just in case. I remember saying, "There's got to be something I can buy," as I excitedly went from cart to cart looking for something to bring home.

What triggers trance spending? Stress, distraction, pretty displays, discounts, feeling tired or low. These are the situations where one can end up with things like hiking poles that "you just had to have," that sit in your closet and never get used.

Filling the Void

While trance spending is pretty unconscious, it's typically an in the moment impulse fueled by distraction. The bigger unconscious motivators driving most spending habits are often more difficult to identify. These can be filling a void of not enough, status anxiety, lifestyle envy, or making a social statement.

In a world where success is determined by where you are on the status continuum, there will always be someone with more or less status than you. According to Alain de Botton in his book *Status Anxiety*, *"status anxiety is the pernicious worry about the danger of failing to conform to the ideals of success laid down by our society."* The resultant anxiety is fueled by feeling that our value and worth is dependent on others' perception of who we are.

"Lifestyle envy" is a trap often created by status anxiety and fed by social media. It holds a tight grip on those trying to maintain a certain appearance for the outside world. Lifestyle envy creates more unhappiness, envy, jealously and self-esteem issues than anything else. The financial strain that people put themselves under in order to keep up with the expectations and lifestyle of those around them removes freedom of choice. Those in its clutches have abdicated, as Victor Frankl in *Man's Search for Meaning* says, "the last of the human freedoms, the freedom to choose one's attitude in any given set of circumstances…to choose one's own way."

Disconnecting from our intrinsic worth creates vulnerability to the myriad of ads designed to perpetuate the message that our value is dependent on who we are and what we have. In these marketing pitches we are told we "deserve it," thus invoking a false sense of entitlement. As a result, we have a lot of stuff. In fact, the average household in America has 300,000 objects. Even though only 3.7% of all the children on the planet live in America, they have 47% of all the toys and books.[14] Money wants to bring us joy, but it doesn't want us to continue to buy "stuff" that only fills our closets and storage units, never bringing us the happiness we hope it will.

The things we own have connections to us; they become extensions of us. They pull on us and hold energy. When we are surrounded by things that we don't really love or that bring us joy, we stay stuck. Worn out and unwanted objects hold stories of other times and places, stories of the places we've been and the things we've done. And they hold stories of who we were, not necessarily who we are now.

My client Sally, a compulsive shopper, was overwhelmed by the burden of debt she'd incurred as a result of her habit. She would often come home with huge bags of clothes that she hid from her husband. While she felt high during her shopping sprees, there was little joy later because each purchase became laden with guilt.

While exploring the part of her who was addicted to shopping, two memories emerged. As a child she didn't fit in, so wearing what the "cool kids" wore was an attempt to find her place in an adversarial environment. Also, the only time she received any attention from her mother was while shopping together. Interestingly, her mother hid her purchases from Sally's father in the same way Sally now did with her husband.

Sally realized that shopping was not about buying more things but about wanting attention, trying to fit in and to feel loved. But her compulsion gave her none of these feelings and only made her feel even worse about herself. Sally spent time healing her inner child who never felt loved. As a result, there wasn't a need to fill hole of unlovability

---

14 http://articles.latimes.com/2014/mar/21/health/la-he-keeping-stuff-20140322

She invited her Money guide to shop with her. When she found herself back in the old shopping trance she heard a little voice saying, "Do you really need this?" Sharing this with me, she laughed and said, "It's as if my Money guide is the voice of reason and I wake back up. I'm now committed to the joy of being debt free, which is slowly becoming a reality."

Trance Withholding vs. Embracing Quality

While there can be trance and mindless spending, there can also be trance withholding. This is where our constrictive fearful parts take over. For example, a friend of mine was planning to make pesto. When confronted with the fact that a small amount of pine nuts was $5.99, he was outraged and decided not to buy them. Instead, he went home and used the pine nuts in the freezer to make his pesto. Unfortunately, they were rancid, but he didn't realize this until the pesto was poured over the hand-made pasta with high-end parmesan, organic basil and extra virgin olive oil. The $5.99 that he didn't spend cost him not only the fresh ingredients he used to make the dinner, but price of eating out, because the meal was inedible and there was nothing in his kitchen to make a new meal. Money does not like a cheap or constrictive attitude. His money was not happy.

My partner was talking to his son about the concept of "trance withholding." He said, "Dad, I totally understand what that means. It's like my situation with Honeycrisp apples. I love Honeycrisps, but they're really expensive, so I often didn't buy them, even though I really like them. I'd go to the store, and instead of buying what I really want, I'd buy a bag of the soft mealy apples that I don't like. I end up with a lot of what I don't want and none of what I do want. If I just bought one Honeycrisp apple and really savored it instead of trying to eat a lot of the mealy apples, I'd really be using my money in a better way." (He's doing that now!)

The cost of something is determined by how much you enjoy and use it. The mealy apples that are cheaper, but not enjoyable, are actually expensive emotionally. In many European countries, value is placed on buying high quality items and using them for a long time. In America, more value is placed on how inexpensive something is and replacing it often. My mother once shared a story of her early days with my father. She grew up in a family that placed a high value on quality. He grew up poor and was taught to focus more on price than quality. He suggested she go to the local bargain basement that sold seconds and discards. Wanting to please, she bought pants and underwear, unaware that the pants were sewn in a way that made them un-wearable. When she washed the underwear, they all disintegrated after a few washes. She said to my father, "How can people who struggle financially afford to buy there? It ends up being really expensive because you have to keep replacing things."

Is there something you've been wanting or yearning for, but you've been telling yourself you can't afford it? Do you spend on little things that you don't really want instead of saving for the thing that you do want? What are the things you "allow" yourself to spend money on and the things you don't, and why? (This goes back to the chapter on receiving)

Money wants to be a source of joy. Constrictive and cheap is not joyful. Neither is mindless spending that is disconnected from true desire.

Mindful Spending

Mindful spending is conscious spending.

One of my biggest takeaways from my years in China is that there are many ways to live a life. I was incredibly happy in my simply furnished home with a view of the river and outlying mountains. I loved what I did and the connections I'd made. I spent my money on the things that were important to me: travel, someone to clean my home, and good food. Since I was clear about where my money would bring the most joy, I still was able to save a large percentage of my income.

My friend, Karen, shared a similar experience of a time when she and her husband lived in France. "I realized that I didn't need to have a lot of things to be happy. We'd put everything in storage and just took the few things that meant the most to us. As I look back on it, it was the connections and experiences we had that brought meaning to our life."

Behavioral economists Elizabeth Dunn and Michael Norton have spent their careers studying the types of spending that brings true happiness. Spending on experiences vs things; sharing and generosity; making spending a "treat;" buying yourself time; and paying now, consuming later are all proven ways to gain greater spending satisfaction. [15]

Mindful spending aligns money's flow with what's truly important to you. As a result, both you and Money are happy. No longer under the influence of outside messages of what you should want or have, there is true freedom and choice. You have nothing to prove to anyone, so what you buy comes from gifting yourself with what your heart truly desires.

My top four values are beauty, adventure, learning and spiritual connection. As a child, I used to dream of a time when I could have fresh flowers every week. As an adult, fresh flowers are as essential a purchase as food. They feed my soul. During times when money was tight, there was still money for flowers, even if it was just one stem in a beautiful little vase. That simple flower brought me as much joy as the luscious bouquets that adorn my home now.

When I first moved to China, all of the expats took taxis. Since one of my values is adventure, taking the bus was not only cheaper, but even

---

15 *Happy Money*, Elizabeth Dunn and Michael Norton

more of an adventure. During peak crowded times, it often felt as if as if I was riding with the sea of Chinese humanity. Still, it was an adventure. I instituted what I called my "bus project." I went to each bus stop within a few blocks of my home and wrote down all the buses that stopped there. I would take a bus, get off at a random spot that looked interesting and explore all the little shops and alleys. When I was ready to head home, I would hop on a different bus with a new route for even more adventure. If I really got lost, there was always the taxi as a backup. My bus adventures were exciting and fun. On top of that, the bus was only ten cents as opposed to five dollars for a taxi.

Do you know what your top four values are? What brings you the most joy and delight? If cooking is your passion, then possibly a few high-quality pots and pans would be something you will use with great joy for a long time. My partner is passionate about his knives. He smiles every time he happily chops with the knives that are precious to him. They bring him great joy.

There are numerous websites where you can determine your top values—I recommend taking the time to do that. After reconnecting to your divine desire, which we explored in a previous chapter, and identifying your values, becoming a conscious, mindful spender will become easier and easier. Your purchases will be satisfying and joy-filled. You won't experience buyer's regret or guilt. Your happy money will be flowing.

The Impact of Mindful Spending

The insatiable consumption that wastes nonrenewable resources doesn't serve us individually or collectively. Today, low price has a high cost. This ethos continues to perpetuate a throwaway society oblivious of the cost to the planet and those who are working in dangerous conditions and living in poverty in order to create a so-called "good deal."

As more people choose products with socially just supply chains that utilize renewable resources, companies will be motivated to create products in ways that promote global generosity and collaboration.

A powerful example of this happened in August of 2019. For decades, corporations have existed primarily to serve shareholders without concern for their impact on other stakeholders. In a *ground-breaking shift,* 181 CEOs signed a new Principles of Corporate Governance pact outlining a modern standard for corporate responsibility. The new principles constitute a commitment to all stakeholders, employees, communities, for fair and ethical treatment of suppliers, sustainable practices for the environment, customers, and investors.[16] Exciting, huh?

It's important to realize this didn't happen in a vacuum. It's a result of our individual efforts having a collective impact by the conscious, mindful decisions we make about how and where we allow our money to flow. By divesting from companies that are socially irresponsible, you're helping to create happy Money in your life and in the world.

---

16 https://www.businessroundtable.org/business-roundtable-redefines-the-purpose-of-a-corporation-to-promote-an-economy-that-serves-all-americans

Dance Steps

1. *Become aware of what is really important to you. Consider the five principals for happy spending: experiences over things; make it a treat; generosity and sharing; buy time; pay now, consume later.*

2. *Take time to determine your values and what is really important to you.*

3. *Bring your Money guide shopping with you. Invite it to support you in your mindful spending practice.*

4. *Continue to thank Money for all the good you have in your life and how Money shows up to support you.*

5. *To break the spell of trance spending, when you are considering a purchase ask yourself, "Do I really need this or do I just want this? If it's a want, what are the feelings I am hoping to get from this? Can I get these feelings in another way that would be even more fulfilling? Do I have the money at this time to buy this? Is this important enough for me that I am willing to figure out how I will get the money?"*

6. *Be conscious of whether what you're buying and who you're buying from are supporting Money to be an agent for good in the marketplace. **Remember, if something wasn't ethically sourced, made, or created, it still holds the energy of exploitation.***

CHAPTER 16

Making Love to the World by Sharing Your Gifts

"Work is love made visible."

Khalil Gibran

One of the ultimate joys in life is the fulfilling expression of our gifts and the realization of our potential. Honoring our gifts and bringing them to the marketplace becomes one of the greatest acts of self-love and caring. As a result, as money flows back to us, it becomes transformed into an expression of joy and fulfillment.

Similarly, Money loves when we hire people to do things they love to do, because we're honoring their gifts. Additionally, Money loves when we invest in companies that are creating sustainable and life-enhancing products and services. Money, in its truest form, wants to be a medium to bring people and cultures together and the expression of our Divinity and love in the marketplace.

Finding Self-Worth in Your Unique Gifts

Each of us comes into this world with our own unique combination of gifts and talents. Even as children those talents begin to find their expression. While one child may spend hours creating a Lego empire, another will be fascinated by bugs and nature. My friend Kate, a very successful entrepreneur, started a little business when she was still in grade school. Her current business is now a multi-million dollar company with a global market. Her talents and passion as an entrepreneur were evident even as a child. Fortunately, her family encouraged and supported her efforts, which gave her the courage and confidence to forge out on her own when the opportunity arose.

Too many budding artists, writers, scientists, actors, and dreamers weren't given support in their home or school environments. Some of the lucky ones will have had someone who believed in them, thus, the encouragement to flourish. For many others, finding their unique place in the world becomes a meandering and often frustrating road to navigate.

For myself, I remember all too well a professor of mine saying to me, "What happened to you? You're so talented, and you just don't see it." Like many, I've struggled with confidence and being able to see and acknowledge my gifts and talents. As a result, it was hard to recognize my value and truly express it in a way that brought the fulfillment I ached for. It is a painful memory, but one that has helped me to have great compassion for those who also struggle to find their own value and worth. I know how painful it can be.

Sadly, during my time in China, many of my students were pushed into areas of study that they had no love or passion for. I remember meeting a young woman who excitedly showed me her beautiful drawings. When I asked her if she was studying art, her expression changed to what seemed like a deep sense of despair. She said, "No, I'm studying accounting." When I asked her why, she told me her mother had decided this for her and her mother knew best. I was empathetic towards her plight, but also understood that stability is an important value in that culture. Unfortunately, it's likely this young woman will never be very successful as an accountant because she has no passion for it.

Navigating through the landscape of life, discovering your calling, and finding meaningful work can be a daunting experience. A common belief is, "Work has to be hard." While there are the few fortunate ones who know their calling at age five, the rest of us sort of bumble along and fall into careers or jobs that have little to do with our passion and purpose. Our gifts are often so innately a part of us that we can be a little like fish who don't realize they are in the water. We don't recognize them as gifts because they come so naturally to us that it's hard to imagine it's not the same for others.

If something is a gift, you'll find ways to express it, no matter where you are. It may not be expressed in a way that brings joy to your heart, but it will eventually leak out. If you are creative, you will tend to approach whatever you do in a way that's creative. Being in an environment that doesn't allow you to explore and try new things will only serve to make you stressed and cranky. Too many rules will feel like prison. This would not be an environment that would allow you to flourish and the money you received from that job would not be happy, joyous money.

On the other hand, if you love structure and details, being in an environment with little structure or rules, with a focus on creativity instead of details, would be difficult. You wouldn't be happy or particularly successful and the money you received from that job would not be happy, joyous money.

I worked with a man who was constantly in a state of angst because he was trying to find his "perfect work." He had a loving wife and family, a beautiful home and, in many ways, his life was an incredible banquet. But all he could focus on was what wasn't working. He was depressed and difficult to be around because his negativity permeated the home.

When, together, we began identifying the qualities in a perfect work week that would be aligned with his joy and delight, he realized that he already had everything he wanted. While his work didn't look like what he "thought" it should look like, it actually gave him a sense of purpose and fulfillment. It utilized his talents and gave him the autonomy he desired. But, because he was so focused on what wasn't working and the package he thought his ideal job should come in, he couldn't recognize that he already had what he'd been searching for.

Constantly being in a state of searching can keep us stuck and unable to see everything that's already working. It's a slippery slide that can lead to a lot of despair. The energy of searching is very different than the energy of finding. Sometimes people are afraid of finding because they unconsciously believe that they'll lose their freedom. For my client, once he realized he'd already had what he was looking for, he felt the sense of freedom he'd been aching for. This is why, as we've explored in earlier chapters, having clean, clear, open receiving channels, a direct connection to true desire, and a transceiver set to the right frequency of sending and receiving is absolutely essential.

Misconstruing Spiritual Expression

When walking a spiritual path, it can be confusing as to what is a "spiritual career"—in other words, a career that supports the expression of one's spirituality. Upon returning to the States, I was confused and frustrated. I didn't want to do what I'd done before, but I had no idea what I did want to do. One day, while meandering through the library, I came across about book by a self-professed "career intuitive." Excitedly, I made an appointment, hoping for the answer to my search. According to her, I was a mystic and could never be successful unless I did the work of a mystic, which was *not* to be found in business. I had no idea what "mystic work" looked like, but in her mind, business and mystics were not congruent. I remember getting off the phone in tears, calling a friend crying, feeling even more confused than before. His response was, "Well, why don't you be a business mystic? I think the world could use more of that." Funny, in many ways I've done just that.

My consultation with the intuitive was an example of putting spirituality, and its expression in the marketplace, into a very tight, small box. Why is it not "spiritual" to create products and services that are of high quality and integrity? What a different world it would be if Money was allowed to express its divinity through all businesses. People would receive a fair wage; they would be encouraged to grow and fulfill themselves; the products they produced would be infused with love and those that bought them would be blessed.

If we intend for money to be an agent of divine love in the marketplace, then that is what it will be. It will be the reflection the highest and best of who we are as a human race. We've created money. We can transform it.

One day, a student raised her hand in a class I was teaching on accessing intuition and guidance and asked, "Do I have a soul contract to have the job I'm in?" She worked in PR for a movie company giving her regular contact with movie stars. For many, it would be a dream job, but she thought she should be doing something more spiritual.

I asked her if she liked her job. She shook her head, yes.

"Do you feel your presence is making a difference?" I asked. She beamed, "It's a stressful job, yet, when I'm around, it seems to calm everyone down."

My response was, "There are many ways to bring your divinity to any situation. Loving your job is the first step. The second is showing up as your best self, shining your light, and making the work environment a better place by your presence."

My student was definitely accomplishing that, so how could she not be walking her souls' path? She was bringing her divinity to the marketplace. How could that not be spiritual?

A dear friend of mine wanted to study comedy. Even though he felt guided to perform comedy he was conflicted because, in his words, "It certainly isn't a spiritual occupation." My response was, "Comedy is one of the most powerful forms of healing we know. Helping people laugh and find humor in a situation is an incredible gift! How could that not be spiritual?" Knowing him, I'm sure that wherever he'd worked in the past (which included Fortune 500 companies), he'd brought a sense of laughter and lightness. Now semi-retired, he can more directly hone his skills as an agent of joy and lightness through stand-up comedy.

My house cleaner, who loves to clean, is raising the vibration of my home and bringing me great joy and delight. My marketing consultant is helping me shine a light so that those I'm called to serve can find me. My book coach is helping me find my voice so that this book can inspire you to have a new relationship with money. Each of them is passionate about their work. The service they provide and the money they're paid ripples out into the marketplace and makes the world a better place. Since we're divine beings, when we honor our gifts and bring a service to the world, we're performing spiritual work.

The Golden Thread

Most careers are not linear. When we listen to our heart, we find ourselves in places we would never imagine, often even better than we imagined. And at the same time, the journey is often one with more than a few trials, experiments or bumps. Our lives are wonderful works of art. You have to be willing to splash paint on the canvas and allow the painting of your life to unfold. You don't have to wait until you "figure it out." It's easier to change the direction of an object in motion than one that is still.

There are many ways to reach a destination, and sometimes destinations change in transit. It is helpful to know where you are going, but if you're not so sure, be assured that you will find a golden thread running through your life.

Ella decided to start a private practice as a psychotherapist after losing her job. She struggled to make her practice lucrative, but it just didn't happen. Not because she isn't a gifted therapist, but because having a business requires a different skill set that she couldn't quite master. After participating in a money retreat, she began to talk to her Money guide who encouraged her to get a job in a group practice. Money wanted her to use her gifts in a way that brought her joy, without experiencing the added stress of finding clients. Today she is happy and financially solid. Both she and her clients are thriving. Instead of celebrating the courage to take the risk, Ella still felt shame and like a failure because she wasn't successful at starting her own business. There is no shame in trying something and deciding you don't want it after all. Too many people never give themselves permission to try out a dream to see if that's their true path. Unfortunately, *the result of never trying is longing, an aching heart, and a lifetime of regret.*

My friend Lindy is a master at creating and adjusting. She decided to quit her corporate job and see what emerged. She spent some months creating art and riding her green, big-wheel bicycle around town with her beloved dog, Baxter, in the front basket. After a time, she opened a wonderful space that had fun, funky, artsy items for sale in the front with a workshop/play space in the back. After two years she decided that, while lots of people loved her place, she wasn't doing her own art and was working way too much for too little return. She closed the store and rented a smaller place to use for workshops and her own studio. She played with a subscription model for funding, but realized that it would take too much time for too little money, so she decided to get a low-stress job and focus on her own art. In all of her decisions she listened to her heart and gave herself permission to take, what felt like, the best next step, no matter what anyone else thought. The queen of manifestation, she got a job with great hours that allows her to express her unique value and gifts. Now she has energy leftover at the end of the day for her creativity to express itself in ways that bring her joy.

One day someone came to me for an Akashic intuitive consult because she was unhappy with her job and wanted guidance as to next best steps. I saw her gifts as beautiful floating orbs of light, aching to have a different form of expression from how they were currently being expressed. Amazed, I sensed that even though her gifts were extensions of her, they were also separate from her. They had an energy and vibration that were a delight to see. Her guides suggested that she find a beautiful container and create an altar for her gifts. She was guided to write the qualities and gifts that she wanted to express in her ideal job on slips of paper and put them in the container. The container represented the perfect expression of those gifts. Even though she didn't know what the job would be, the guides instructed her to begin calling it to her. They instructed her to light a candle daily and talk to her gifts, to send them blessings and invite them to find the work that would allow them to be more fully present in the world and in her life. Shortly thereafter she found a wonderful job with less stress—one that gave her more passion than she ever imagined.

Taking Back Your Power of Choice

So, what to do if you find yourself in a soul-sucking job and you feel as if you have no other options? Instead of focusing on what you hate about your job, re-empower yourself by bringing choice into the situation. First, notice the job and take a moment to give thanks for the fact that it's paying the bills. Bless the job, bless all the people there, and make a commitment to show up as your best self. Then, give thanks for the new job that will feed your soul and believe that it's on the way to you. Trust the process, even though you don't know what it is or when it'll show up. Praying as if your prayer has already been answered is key to drawing it to you.

I shared this quote in the last chapter but it feels appropriate to share it again: "The last of the human freedoms – is the ability to choose one's attitude in any given set of circumstances."[17] This was the wisdom Victor Frankl developed as a result of his time in a concentration camp, witnessing the attitude of those who survived its horrors and those who didn't. This freedom to choose your attitude is always available to you and can be exercised in any situation, even in a soul-sucking job. If so, you will grow both emotionally and spiritually.

New Opportunities in a New Economy

Today there are more ways for money to be shared and created than ever before. Despite its challenges, the sharing economy has broadened opportunities and turned strangers into friends. Artists and creatives, who traditionally were pushed into "day jobs," now have access to a global market, including indigenous artisans who are able to maintain traditional art forms that might have been otherwise lost. The idea of an economic system that is collaborative and generous is starting to become not only a possibility, but a reality.

One of my favorite stories is of a young Nigerian man who grew up poor with a dream to become a successful blogger. He began to study bloggers and to blog himself. Over time, he established a freelance writing career and is now teaching people his keys to success and earning multiple six figures, proving we're not limited by where we live. There are numerous examples of those who travel the world and still connect with their audience. All they need is a device and access to the internet.

---

17 Victor Frankl, *Man's Search for Meaning.*

New legal entities are being created for companies whose main purpose is to develop products and services that significantly add to the social good of the world. The internet has leveled the playing field for many who otherwise would not have had access to the financial opportunities it affords. Crowd funding sites provide capital for new ideas that might never have come to market. Today, with a laptop and internet access, someone in a small town anywhere in the world can open their home to tourists looking for an intimate cultural connection that would never have been possible in the past.

Choosing From a Position of Empowerment

Make your decisions from a place of choice and empowerment, not from fear. The more people entering the marketplace who choose work based on purpose and meaning, the more purpose and meaning will drive the market. Thankfully, many young people today are making these choices. They're not willing to stay in jobs just for the money.[18] As a result, numerous companies are now hiring consultants to assist them to identify and hire people who are purpose-driven as opposed to those who just want a job. These employees are more committed, bringing more of their best self to their work.

Expressing your divinity and magnificence is the most important thing you can do. Bless your gifts, your life, your money and yourself. Bless your future and welcome its perfect expression of your highest good. Know you are a spiritual being having a human experience. Bring the highest compassion and love to yourself. Doing this will give you more ability to play and enjoy the sweetness of life and allow you to share it with others. Commit to honor the divinity in all creation and allow Money to express that divinity through you.

---

18 https://www.forbes.com/sites/karlmoore/2014/10/02/millennials-work-for-pur-pose-not-paycheck/#78156aee6a51

The following is a prayer that was given to me as a gift to the world. Feel free to share it! Saying it daily as you explore your next steps is a gift you can give to yourself.

Prayer for Perfect Expression of Gifts

I ask now that my mind, body and spirit be aligned for my talents and gifts to coalesce into their perfect divine expression in the marketplace.

Let me step forward with confidence, ease and grace. May my magnificence shine as brightly as a star, illuminating the way for those I am called to serve.

May I flourish in all ways—financially, emotionally, physically and spiritually as I open my heart to receive, in joyous delight, all the good that life has to offer.

Dance Steps

As you ponder what is next, here are some steps you can take that may help you gain clarity on your unique gifts and their expression.

1. *Considering we don't always see ourselves so clearly, it can be helpful to interview people who can see you in a way you may not be able to see yourself. I recommend calling a few people you trust. The following are questions you may want to consider:*

   1. *What do you see as my greatest gifts?*
   2. *What do you see as my strengths?*
   3. *What are three different ways you could imagine me expressing these gifts and strengths?*

2. *Find mentors, helpers, and others who have done what you want to do. Study how they've done it. Surround yourself with people who inspire you, who see you, and who are taking action toward their dreams. They will motivate you to do the same. Know that if one person has done what you're aspiring to do, you can do it, too. Maybe not in the same way as them, but it will be uniquely you.*

3. *Like the woman who was guided to create an altar for her gifts, you can do the same. Find a beautiful container that will represent the perfect expression of your gifts in the marketplace. Write down all of the gifts you want to express on slips of paper and place them in your container. Light a candle and talk to your gifts daily, inviting them to guide you to the perfect job or work. If you get an intuitive hit to do something, go somewhere, or talk to someone, do it! Expect miracles and you will get them. Also, be open for things to come to you in ways you wouldn't expect.*

4. *For more in-depth gift exploration, go to Brian Jaudon's site, https://www.livinggiftconsciousness.org*

CHAPTER 17

Dancing in Joy, Delight and Enough

"...find out where joy resides, give it a voice far beyond singing. For to miss the joy is to miss all."

Robert Louis Stevenson

He who knows that enough is enough will always have enough.

Lao Tzu

Anyone who knows me or has worked with me is aware that I am passionate about joy and delight. That being said, the original title of this book was, *Money, a Healing Journey*. Not very joyful, huh? Sort of like most people's relationship with money. I knew that just exploring the topic of money could be heavy and I wanted to infuse it with a sense of lightness. My questions were: Can we play at this? Can we make it fun? What if we made it a dance? Yes! A dance!

A few years ago, I was a passenger in what should have been a fatal car accident on a country road in France. We were hit by a delivery truck at 80 miles an hour. Days later, while giving my deposition, the officer taking it shook his head back and forth-- murmuring in French, "You should be dead."

In the time since, the preciousness of the dance of life and the importance of living in delight has grown stronger in me. In my work with Money, the message I've continually received is "Love, joy, and delight are our birthright."

The purpose of this book has been to invite you to dance with Money, so that you can begin to live with joyous wealth and well-being, remembering that you are the beloved creation of a Divine Creator. You are deeply and dearly loved, always have been, always will be. You are Divine. You are enough. This is your original innocence.

Your divinity did not disappear because you took on human form. Being human is not easy. But it is precisely why we choose to be in a body—to learn, to grow, to be tested. As a result, we forget the truth of our divinity. Our pain and struggle with money are the indicators of how much we've forgotten that truth. This is the human journey, to forget and to remember.

Remembering our original innocence is our voyage back to Divine Source. Grace, comfort, peace, expansion, generosity, delight and much more live here, as does our connection to all of creation.

During one of my travels I had an experience of profound generosity. On a small wooden boat at sunset deep in the Amazon jungle, our Achuar guide, a short man with dark hair and a large toothy smile, deftly guided us through the water. The cool breeze gave a welcome relief from the heat of the day. As darkness descended, he turned off the motor. In the silence, the jungle came alive. It was as if I could feel it breathe. It was a powerful, undulating breath teaming with life—not only the life of the plants, animals, and everything else that inhabits the jungle, but also the deep breath of the Earth itself.

This breath, that I felt so deeply, is a generous breath. It is the lungs of our beloved planet. It breathes on behalf of all life. In that moment, I understood to my core the preciousness of this Earth we call home and the interconnectedness of all creation. I felt a deep sense of belonging to something larger than me. As the jungle breathed, I breathed. We breathed together.

The fundamental truth of creation is that its very existence is an act of generosity. Creation is intelligent, inspirational, and adaptive. It is interdependent and collaborative. It knows beauty and awe.

How is it that we humans, who are supposedly the pinnacle of this creation, have strayed so far from our own true potential? We are creators and innovators. We must become the stewards of our enormous potential, inviting our most generous and best selves into all that we do. This includes inviting Money, our creation, to be an agent for good, aligned with collaboration and generosity, the new matrix of humanity.

It starts with each one of us, the choices and decisions we make, the people we vote into power, how we spend, and how generous we are with ourselves and others. Generosity and collaboration are an attitude and a way of being. Holding a vision of the new world we want and becoming the change we desire to see in that world sets up an energetic matrix. Collectively, our conscious choices support the new paradigm of humanity and money. This is true wealth—for you, your global neighbors and the planet. It is not who we were, but who we are becoming.

> *Money, come dance with me. Dance with me in my humanity and divinity, as an expansive creator being, as conscious mindful flow, as a love-maker in the marketplace, as generosity, as joy, as wealth, as delight, as a rewriter of stories, as a healer and healed one. Money, as the expression Divine Source, come dance with me. Help me to know that I am enough and enough is enough, that there will always be enough and more than enough. I embrace and celebrate the garden of earthly delights as the gift of the Divine. Help me to honor myself, You, and all creation. Knowing that in the asking it is received, I give heartfelt thanks. And, so it is.*

Thank you for the opportunity to dance this dance with you and Money. May your dances be always Divinely guided.

Blessings,
Gale

Acknowledgements

I'd like to thank all the teachers, mentors and guides in both the seen and unseen realms who have gifted me with their wisdom and guidance throughout my life.

I want to give special thanks to my friend and mentor, Richard Schwartz, who had the courage to not only develop the Internal Family Systems Model, but to also include the concept of spiritual guidance. To friend and mentor, Greg Johansen, of the Hakomi Institute who shared with me the sensitivity cycle of creation. To Ellena Leiberman, my teacher in the Akashic Records. To my book coaches and editors, Sally Stone, Kim O'Hara, and Katie Boyle. To fellow Akashic Record consultants, Francesca Thoman and Tara Joli, with whom I shared my early communication with Money. To all of the clients and workshop participants I've had the privilege to work with over the years. To my partner, Mark Hurwich, who has supported me in so many ways. To all those who encouraged me when I became discouraged. And to you, the reader, for taking the journey.

Resources

Achor, Shawn. *Before Happiness: the 5 Hidden Keys to Achieving Success, Spreading Happiness, and Sustaining Positive Change.* 2013

Dunn, Elizabeth & Norton, Michael. *Happy Money: The Science of Happier Spending.* 2014

Earley, Jay. *Self-Therapy: A Step by Step Guide to Creating Wholeness and Healing Your Inner Child Using IFS, A New, Cutting Edge Psychotherapy,* Second Edition. 2012

Emmons, Robert. *Thanks!: How the New Science of Gratitude Can Make You Happier.* 2017

Gober, Mark. *Dispelling the Myth that the Brain Produces Consciousness and the Implications for Every Day Life.* 2018

Goldhamer, Douglas & Bagley, Peggy. *Healing with God's Love: Kabbalah's Hidden Secrets.* 2015

Hawkins, Deborah. *Practice Gratitude: Transform Your Life: Making the Uplifting Practice of Gratitude Intentional.* 2019

Honda, Ken. *Happy Money: The Japanese Art of Making Peace with Your Money.* 2019

Kelley, Tim. *True Purpose: 12 Strategies for Discovering the Difference You Are Meant to Make.* 2009

Laszlo, Ervin. *Science and the Akashic Field: An Integral Theory of Everything.* 2007

Laszlo, Ervin. *The Intelligence of the Cosmos: Why Are We Here? New Answers From the Frontiers of Science.* 2017

Lee, Ingrid Fetell. *Joyful: The Surprising Power of Ordinary Things to Create Extraordinary Happiness.* 2018

Loving, L. Hunter & Wallis, Stewart & Wijkman, Anders & Fullerton, John. *A Finer Future: Creating An Economy In Service To Life.* 2018

Mossbridge, Julia. *The Calling: A 12-Week Science Based Program to Discover, Energize, and Engage Your Soul's Work.* 2019

Nani, Christel. *Sacred Choices: Thinking Outside the Tribe to Heal Your Spirit.* 2006

Needleman, Jacob. *Money and the Meaning of Life.* 1994

Peele, Brandon. *Planet on Purpose: Your Guide to Genuine Prosperity, Authentic Leadership and a Better World.* 2018

Perkins, John. *New Confessions of an Economic Hitman.* 2016

Perkins, John. *Shapeshifting, Shamanic Techniques for Global and Personal Transformation.* 1997

Perkins, John. *The World Is As You Dream It: Teachings From the Amazon and Andes.* 1994

Rutte, Martin. *Project Heaven on Earth: The 3 Simple Questions that Will Help You Change the World...Easily.* 2018

Salk, Jonas, & Salk, Johnathon. A *New Reality: Human Evolution for a Sustainable Future.* 2018

Schwartz, Richard C. *Introduction to the Internal Family Systems Model.* 2001

Weisman, Richard. *The Luck Factor: The Scientific Study of the Lucky Mind.* 2011

Wilkinson, Richard & Pickett, Kate. *The Spirit Level: Why Greater Equality Makes Societies Stronger.* 2010